Daily Spiritual Insight

365 Lessons
for
Lifetime Growth

DANIELLE EGNEW

To Ella ~
May The Healer
Find Healing!
♥

Printed in the United States of America
Copyright © 2014 Danielle Egnew

ISBN-10: 1500202444
ISBN-13: 9781500202446

Cover photographs: Rebecca Douglas
Cover design: Danielle Egnew

Published by Create Space with permission from
The Call To Light Press
A division of Ave Vox Entertainment Group
15021 Ventura Blvd Suite 843, Sherman Oaks, CA 91403
contact@avevoxentertainment.com

Danielle Egnew, Billings, MT

DEDICATION

To all those who seek.
May you find.

And to Rebecca.
So glad you are found.

CONTENTS

As a Psychic and Medium, a large part of my work is translation. I translate between my clients and the spiritual realm that wishes to communicate with them. Though this book is not a work translated from the ethers, but instead contains my own summations and observations of spiritual journeys and lessons, I would not have been able to compile this book without my extensive work with Angelic entities in particular.

My work with Angels has been not only been an enlightening experience but a humbling one. Angels are not like people. Humans don't die and become Angels, though we often like to envision our loved ones as our "guardian angel". Angels are their own spiritual genus, a race of beings created to multi-task across many dimensions and timelines. They are fierce rather than fluffy though their very fabric is woven of Peace and Love. They don't struggle with right or wrong. They don't labor over finding their moral center because there is no "moral" when there is only "light. They have no need for evaluating "grey area" and they don't understand our choice to experience pain in order to learn yet they accept this tendency as a predominant human trait. They cannot fathom why we choose the illusion of isolation from Creation and they don't understand why human beings struggle with the idea of receiving love as they *are* love and they have no concept of self-loathing. Angels are pure Universal truth, justice and creation. They have no opinion. That's a human need. They are function, form, and forward motion. They are builders, sometimes destroying to build again. For Angels, every action is all about the reaction. They manage multi-dimensional chaos like sorting the mail.

When translating for these wonderful and very on-point beings, it's important to remember one thing: They don't speak human. Not in any way, shape, or form. My job, as a translator is to frame up their many concepts, hints, pieces of advice, and guidance in a way that is humanly palatable, which basically means adding some heart, some fallible cultural references, an analogy or two, and a little humor -- something Angels simply lack by our funny bone standards. The only thing we truly share with Angels is our ability to love. Though Angels are all love, theirs is a different type of affection, so white-hot and pure that it often remains undetectable on the struggling human emotional scale. I've learned a great deal about language while working with Angelic entities. Every word we speak in this incarnation, this edgy third dimension, carries vibration and weight. Every word becomes a currency of sorts which purchases our next experience. Indeed, words matter more than we realize. Our Angelic friends, being messengers, are highly aware of this. I've become a much better communicator thanks to my work with these entities. And thanks to this work, my outlook on life here on Earth has dramatically changed.

Emotional situations that we often consider do-or-die, make-or-break, do not even come up on the Angelic radar as remotely significant. This fascinating dichotomy between the significance we assign to our crippling emotional response to pain, and Angelic dismissal of this same trauma as utter minutia in our life trajectory, then triggered a realization within me: Everyday, we make mountains out of mole hills that then become continents warring with one another. We create our own hell. We stub our toe for a moment and decide the pain should not simply be in the toe, but a lifelong full-body process. We choose suffering as a means to learn. And we don't have to.

In fact, we can change our life completely, simply by changing one item a day -- then really *deciding* to accept the change we've enacted.

That's what this book is all about.

Daily life doesn't allow much time for reflection. Many of us are working more than one job, supporting a family, even going back to school. The list of daily items that occupy our time is enormous. Many have endured horrible life events that have left deep scars that they struggle to overcome, all the while juggling a disjointed daily routine that commands our fading focus. Though it would be an amazing experience to sit atop a mountain and meditate on life's meaning -- most of us don't have that type of vacation time accrued. Not to mention the cost of parking oneself in a mountain resort for an entire year.

This book is about realistically making changes within your spirit and your psyche -- starting right where you are today. One lesson at a time. One day at a time. One decision at a time. Focus on the lesson for the day and that lesson only. Put the lesson for the day to use. Allow 24 hours to let it sink in. Then allow a lifetime for the lesson to blossom.

Change is a decision and then an action. I've learned it's that simple.

You can do this.

~~

.

DAY 1
EMOTIONAL SENIORITY

Our emotions are complicated yet our spirit is simple. Our spirit desires love yet our head complicates both giving and receiving love. Our spirit desires peace yet our head complicates peaceful situations. Considering we are a spirit first, then born into the body -- our spirit was here first. The spirit, not the flesh, has emotional seniority. Always lead with your spirit.

It's been around the block and it knows what it's doing.

DAY 2
VOCABULARY LESSON

When you're told that your dreams are impractical, just own the word: "I'Mpractical!" When you're told your goals are improbable, own the word: "I'Mprobable!" And when you're told that your path is impossible, just remember:

"I'M POSSIBLE!"

DAY 3
MAKING ASSUMPTIONS

We must watch our tendency to make assumptions. There really is very little difference between an "assumption" and a "delusion". Assumptions are nothing more than a blank canvas within the mind, ready to receive upon it any image we wish to create. If we are continuously authoring negative, conspiracy-like assumptions -- or images in our mind --we must ask ourselves: What am I attempting to work out INSIDE OF ME by casting others in the role of the oppressor, the user, the manipulator, the liar, etc. What INSIDE OF ME is the oppressor, the user, the manipulator, the liar? We accuse others of that which we are thoroughly capable of doing. That's why we fear someone else will do it to us. So before you assign motive to someone's actions -- try asking first, to clarify. Nine times out of ten, the assumption you've projected onto that person exists as a fear only in your mind. Assumptions don't only "make an ass out of you and me". They ruin friendships, relationships, business deals -- all because one person committed to their own illusion in an attempt to control their surroundings. After all, that's what an assumption is:

A script written by a person who must know the outcome of a situation so badly -- they create it themselves.

DAY 4
UNDERSTANDING DOUBT

Without doubt, there would never be self-exploration. Doubt is not always a harbinger of a poor choice or a foreboding "foreshadow" of a wrong move. Often, doubt is a sign that you're pushing yourself past your usual comfort level into new territory. Doubt is a road sign at a forked intersection that reads: "CONGRATULATIONS! You've turned an important corner!" Don't be discouraged by your doubt. Be inspired to investigate the emotion further.

You can't find the treasure if you never dig beneath the sand.

DAY 5
WHAT TRAPS US?

Darkness is unable to directly affect Light. Instead, it must continually whisper to us, deep from the recesses of our own doubt, playing on our insecurities until we begin to believe the illusion it is attempting to project onto our consciousness. If we buy into this illusion-distorted version of our life -- of ourselves -- then we are not trapped by Darkness itself --

-- but trapped by our own participation with it.

DAY 6
IDENTIFYING BLOCKS

Sometimes the most obvious course of action is to take the opposite action of any action that is not producing the intended results. Though the Universe will not oppose us, it will not incarnate into something that is not intended for us. Like in a maze, "Dead Ends" are not dead. They are simply indicators that we are moving in the wrong direction. There is always a way in and a way out. Rather than pushing against the unintended path, or the "brick wall", take a few steps back, and re-check your options for direction. Chances are, to get the point of termination, you passed many open pathways. Once we release the idea that we must create a direction where one is not intended, we are suddenly made aware of the many options for movement around us. We are not blocked by this life.

We are blocked by our own insistence that we are blocked.

DAY 7
ACCEPTANCE

When the going gets tough --

-- the tough accept that Spirit is in charge.

DAY 8
SHINE BRIGHTLY

If you're feeling down, try this: Shining brightly. No matter how crummy you feel, pick one thing you can do today – for another person. And do it. No matter how downtrodden, depressed, wronged, or under the weather you feel – do one kind thing for another individual, preferably someone that has nothing to do with any sort of turmoil you are personally experiencing, and cause them joy. Call someone and leave a voicemail that you love them just because. Bring an office mate a coffee. Do something kind for another that they are not expecting, that is above and beyond their daily routine. The repercussions of this action, the choice to disassociate ourselves from our own pain in order to bring levity to someone else, brings immeasurable healing to our spirit in ways that we are unaware that we even require. Part of picking ourselves up and dusting ourselves off has to do with dusting ourselves off spiritually. We may not be able to change how someone else chooses to treat us. But we can definitely change how we choose to treat someone else. By enacting kindness to a third-party, we create a vibration of kindness within ourselves.

Within kindness, there is peace.

DAY 9
LOVE YOURSELF

LOVE is the most powerful force in the universe. People fall into ugliness because they fear that they are not loved for who they really are. Often, we don't even love ourselves because we believe that we don't deserve it. We believe we are not worthy of love until we are perfect. Considering we were never designed to be perfect, yet we were designed to be loved, one cannot be attached to the other. If you find that you're having difficulty loving yourself, at least start with attempting to LIKE yourself.

After all, if other people like you -- then allow yourself to be led by example!

DAY 10
UNDERSTANDING DESPERATION

Desperation is a blindness of the spirit brought on by fear. Acting out of desperation for any reason nets temporary results. When you find yourself making associations because you're not getting what you seek "fast enough", be they personal or professional, you end up not getting what you seek anyway. If you seek balanced partnership yet desperation drives you to marry the first person to come along regardless of your compatibility, the partnership is not balanced though you have achieved marriage. Desperation camouflages the path that is attempting to lay itself at your feet. Desperation clouds your decision-making, convincing you that the weakest of choices and associations is the only option. There is no ONLY option.

Desperation will do its best to convince you otherwise.

DAY 11
CAST IN ROLES

We cannot decide how others choose to categorize us. We can decide how to interact with those who choose to interact not with us, but with their idea of us that furthers their own needs. We are not props in the drama of someone else's struggle with themselves, their life choices, or their difficulties with other relationships. We are not obligated to wear the villain costume draped upon our back because others crave the distraction of a singular external focus for their cumulative internal unrest. Those who create distance in their relationships by regularly casting villains in their life play are those who within -- are their worst villain.

There is no making peace with unacknowledged darkness.

DAY 12
QUALITY OF LIFE

It's not where you live, but *how* you live, that defines the quality of your life. No matter the size of your home, what debt you may carry, if your car runs, or what neighbors you may have -- *how* you choose to experience each day defines your lifestyle, not the brand on your sunglasses.

Your JOY is not for sale.

DAY 13
THE ROLE OF COMPASSION

The human race, without compassion, lacks the capacity to govern itself with dignity. Without dignity, the human race lacks the capacity to respect the individual. Without respect for the individual, we lack the capacity to find value in the Self. Without finding value in the Self, we lack relevance to one another and our surroundings. Without relevance, we have no need for forgiveness. Without forgiveness, the human race cannot learn compassion. The key to the next phase of human consciousness is embracing that most basic operating system upon which all other functions depend: Compassion.

Without compassion, the evolution of our species is simply not possible.

DAY 14
ACCOUNTABILITY HEALS

When it's time to point the finger of blame at no one but yourself, make sure to include the rest of your hand to pat yourself on the back.

Accountability heals.

DAY 15
RIDE THE CURRENT

Allow the current of life to take you when the trade winds of opportunity stop blowing. The Flow is a more faithful navigator than the maps we diligently chart our course upon. It's the Spiritual Nature of energy to seek the path of least resistance.

It's the Human Nature of energy to seek resistance along the path.

DAY 16
WATCH THE LEAVES

When it's all "too much" -- watch leaves fall. There's much to be learned. The leaf was once a hyper-important part of the tree's growth, being the very thing that created the photosynthesis that kept the enormous tree alive. The leaf likely provided shelter for many a bird and squirrel, shaded a hiker or two, and even fed a few insects. Yet it is not the tree, nor the bird, nor the squirrel, nor the insect, nor the hiker that keeps the leaf alive. It is light -- the light of the sun. When the days shorten, the leaf shrivels and dies in the elongated darkness of fall. Then, with the ease of the wind, this once pivotal component catches flight, floating to the ground, becoming the very mulch that warms the tree roots against the first frost so the sap may run back to the ground and the tree may safely go dormant until spring. Even in its death, the leaf serves a purpose unto another. In life, we are the leaves -- impermanent in our life cycle, serving many purposes and affecting so much, unable to live without The Light, and with the change in the wind, we are put to rest in the earth. We may look at the leaf and think, "How short and tragic a life." Or, we can see the journey from another perspective: Stuck to the tree, to the insect, to the bird and squirrel, until given the opportunity to take flight with a change in the wind.

When it's all "too much" -- watch leaves fall. There's much to be learned.

DAY 17
DESTINY

Do not focus on the stumbling blocks in your path as there will always be cause to stumble. Instead, raise your eyes to the horizon and keep a steady pace, for the one who is able to stay the course no matter how paved with obstacles --

-- is the one whose path is laid by destiny.

DAY 18
THE BIG PICTURE

Rather than wondering if you even factor into life's "Grand Plan" , try adjusting your perception to wrap your brain around the fact that the Grand Plan was designed specifically -- to factor in and work around *your* gifts. We each hold a piece to the puzzle. Are you taking the time to sit at the table and add your piece? FYI -- the person to your right just may have the piece that is dependant on your puzzle placement. We each are an intricate aspect of the Grand Design. NO piece is greater than the other.

Yet each is required for the big picture to come into focus.

DAY 19
BEING HUMAN

Being Human is a gift. It's the gift of choice, the gift of learning, the gift of laughter and the gift of loving. Sometimes the Human condition involves great pain. But through great pain, great understanding is achieved. To hurt is Human, to heighten is Human, and to heal is Human.

Our time here is short but our impact on the future lasts indefinitely.

DAY 20
ABUNDANCE

Abundance is not simply about "how much" of any one thing you have. It's also about how readily it is available. An abundant life is a life full of avenues that fill you up when you need filling. To practice the Law of Abundance is to practice Accepting in the Moment. We cannot stockpile love, compassion, someone listening to our woes, hugs, beautiful romantic moments, an uncontrollable giggle session -- these things must be received and appreciated in the moment. To be "in abundance" means we are an open turnstile that allows the energy to flow in and out of our lives. Abundance is a sense of abandon, a state of being, the openness to receive in the moment that does not require a full bank account or a new car as proof of its existence. One can be abundant and lack prosperity. One can be prosperous and lack abundance.

Abundance is the willingness -- and excitement -- to receive.

DAY 21
PURPOSE

Where there is great peace --

-- there is great purpose.

DAY 22
BE!

BE warm, BE big, let your light glow, and gift your love to the world! Allow your compassion and uplifting spirit to splash every surface you touch. Those who recoil from your light have the right to do so just as you have the right to shine and be shined upon. It is not our responsibility to dim our radiance for the convenience of others. Nor is it our duty to cool ourselves when others fear our warmth. Those who are most comfortable in the dark cannot relate with the warmth of the light anyway.

Shine with no expectations, and watch your world open.

DAY 23
ANGER

It's okay to get angry sometimes. It's just not healthy for any one of us to let anger eat us alive or become a permanent vehicle for our pain, disappointment, or fear. Pain and fear sharpen anger into a deadly weapon. Darkness then exploits the emotion. But anger in its purest form, coupled with discernment and temperance, can be a tremendous motivator --

-- a powerful catalyst for change.

DAY 24
SPIRITUAL DESIGN

The more you fight your nature, the more nature will fight you. Embrace your spiritual design. You are just right for where you are supposed to be, right now, in your life. Have faith that you are "enough" for any given situation. Rest in the Peace that is secured by who you are --

-- and the Grace (unearned "slack") that is secured for you by your Creator.

DAY 25
DECEPTION

To willingly dance to the tune of deception makes one a partner in the movement, even if one did not write the music. Choose all associations with dignity and based upon your own experience rather than desperation and flattery. To judge or ostracize others is to grant permission to everyone to do the same to you. Have Faith that The Truth of YOU is enough and stand behind Truth in others. Leave illusion and conjecture to those who still wrestle with the identity of who they truly are. Choosing self-discovery through participating in deception is a painful path to walk.

Have compassion for those who choose this journey.

DAY 26
LEARNING CURVE

Humans require contrast in order to learn. Yet It isn't about what we do or don't do. It's about how we choose to respond to what others do or don't do. Our actions are a reflection of how we think. Our response to others' actions are a reflection of how we feel. The moment we realize that none of "it" is actually about "us" --

-- the clearer the path to learning without creating polarizing situations to do so.

DAY 27
PERMISSION

We can only "dummy down" who we are for others or for a situation for so long before life will demand we rise to our own occasion. Becoming less of ourselves so that others may feel more confident in bringing more of themselves into the world is effective in small doses while assisting in building another's confidence. Yet it's not the way to live out one's life. If we must continually "edit" our needs, our gifts, and our personality so that others are made comfortable to be around us, we are not only selling ourselves short, but selling others short in assuming they cannot handle all that we are.

Shining brightly gives others permission to do so as well.

DAY 28
CAUSE AND EFFECT

Our choices today define our future. Our conscience defines our choices. Our heart defines our conscience. Our spirit defines our heart.

Set your spirit right and the rest will follow.

DAY 29
SPIRITUAL TOOL CHEST

When you look back at your life seeing only disappointments and regrets and you feel like you've got nothing left to build upon -- it's time to do an inventory of your Spiritual Tool Chest. See that ratchet, the one labeled "extra heavy duty sense of self"? You obtained that when you had to tighten up some life-or-death leaks in your heart. How about that Sharpie marked "Healthy Boundaries" that you whipped out when it was time to draw the line? Or that ten pound ball peen hammer marked "Inspiration" you picked up to drive the last nail in the coffin of a dysfunctional situation? Thanks to the challenges life has thrown us, our arsenal of tools we've collected in order to fix each broken situation, one at a time -- is now an unstoppable warehouse full of possibility in our hands. We now have a tool for every job, every challenge. The dings in your armor aren't a weakness. They're a reminder that no matter how many times you're knocked off your horse, you have a tool in that enormous warehouse just to patch that breast plate --

-- no matter what caused it to crack.

DAY 30
EMOTIONAL PAIN

Emotional pain is a sign post pointing toward an issue that needs removal from our psyche. We must occasionally choose to sit with our own pain, without distraction, to realize where its point of origin is rooted within us. Like the swollen flesh surrounding a sliver to drive it out, our "pain" surrounds the emotional issue within that needs releasing.

Don't fear the sign post. It points to the direction of healing.

DAY 31
HYPOSCRISY

Honesty and accountability are often the most difficult tools to find within ourselves yet we demand those tools be used when others wish to build upon our emotional property. If you're not willing to lend your tools to another who may be lacking, who are you to demand that another invest in you? We cannot expect to receive that which we do not give.

Give freely and receive freely.

DAY 32
HEAD VS HEART

Within our spirit lies our compassion. Our mind can rationalize the mechanics of unkindness yet our spirit cannot. Our head must present a case to our heart with the precision of an attorney when attempting to convince our heart to hold a grudge, hate, distrust -- become bitter. The heart is never truly able to accomplish these feats but only steps aside as the head is allowed to rationalize these actions into existence. The heart then suffers as its connection to life around it is interrupted. We cannot separate our heart from our spirit. We cannot separate our spirit from Creation / Universe / God. Creator is all things. By the very nature of our spirit we cannot separate ourselves from ALL THINGS. We are each other, in the heart. We are the ocean, the mountains, the sunset -- in the heart.

Once we accept "we are" we must accept that there is no such thing as "us against them".

DAY 33
IMPOSSIBILITY

Whatever you feel is impossible for you to accomplish -- turn all your energies toward this endeavor. It is in climbing our own mental mountains that we are able to conquer the numerous flat lands beyond. Before we can claim dominion over our path --

-- we must claim dominion over our fears.

DAY 34
THE FUTURE

Knowing "what's going to happen in the future" is a slippery slope. At the end of each day it doesn't matter who said what, who did what, or if the sky falls like Chicken Little said it would. At the end of each day, what matters is who you chose to be -- that day. This single action defines your tomorrow. Our choices in attitude sculpt our emotional landscaping day to day. We design our moods. No one has control over how you feel except you. It's not what life throws at you and why. It's how you handle it all that matters.

You can do it.

DAY 35
OPPORTUNITY

Where there is struggle there is great opportunity to make new choices. Where there are new choices --

-- the opportunities are endless.

DAY 36
HATE

Hate is a one-dimensional emotion and can only exist if its subject is viewed from one angle -- as a concept. Compassion requires 3-D viewing. Hate is the generic dirty sheet we throw over a person, place, or issue now soiled by wrestling with our own challenges. We relegate whatever is beneath the sheet to become the same faceless yet recognizable target, again and again.

As an emotion, hate must chase ghosts to survive.

DAY 37
TEAMWORK

Nothing we accomplish is without the assistance of others. Just when you leave the house thinking you're the "only one doing the work", be reminded that a cafe attendant made the coffee that you purchased after you pulled out of your driveway that the construction crew poured years before. If humanity can unconsciously support itself everyday --

-- imagine what we can do once we DECIDE to be of use?

DAY 38
SIGNS

Have you asked, "Why doesn't God give me a sign?" The Universe provides us with wonderful prompts, hints, and signs all the time. Unfortunately, we don't often take the cue from the sign, and we then require the Universal two-by-four between the eyes. Next time you say to the Universe, "show me a sign", perhaps the request should be: "Allow me to accept the sign I'm asking to be shown." This will save you from plenty of Karmic shiners down the road. We see the signs. We just don't believe they apply to us. Which is why Highway Patrolmen everywhere make their ticket quotas each month as drivers across the nation disregard sign after sign that read "Speed Limit 65".

Surely those signs are for someone else...

DAY 39
FEAR

Fear is a time bandit, robbing the future of hope. Fear is an illusion, and a powerful tool that Darkness relies on humanity to use against itself. As long as we allow ourselves to be preoccupied by the crippling effects of fear, we will be trapped inside our own minds, fighting our own worst case scenarios, instead of stepping forward outside of our own thoughts to make the real-world changes that will rob fear of any footing in our lives. To recognize "the power of fear" for the illusion that it is means to recognize our OWN power to create such a powerful illusion. Re-channel all of that enormous power into positive everyday steps toward positive change. We must recognize that we, not fear, are our own captors. We, ourselves, are the very incubator that births fear into our world. We are not the victims of fear, but its creators. Once we free ourselves from our own power to create negatively, and activate our power to create positively --

-- we unshackle our life path from our own demons.

DAY 40
SPREAD LOVE

Today, make sure to tell the people that are in your life that YOU LOVE THEM. We will never know the pain of another's journey. Life is a fragile and short thing. No matter how much time has passed since you've seen them, or how much water may be under the bridge --

-- all that matters is that you let those in your life know they are loved.

DAY 41
RESENTMENT

It's interesting how the human species will treat those closest to us with the least regard. Or, hang all of our fears on that close person even if the fears don't exist. We test out our own worst nightmares on others -- creating horrors for all involved. When a loved one treats another poorly, it's an indication that they resent themselves, and conversely, resent the person who cares about them for doing so. If you find yourself constantly snapping at someone who is delivering love and kindness to you, ask yourself: What do I resent in myself? Then -- forgive yourself for what you find.

Without self-forgiveness, we can truly never be free to love another, as our primary relationship will be with our own resentment.

DAY 42
CHALLENGE

The best blessings--

-- come disguised as challenges.

DAY 43
GRATITUDE

Thank others for their goodness -- many will not notice. Have gratitude for the contributions of those who have touched your life -- most will take them for granted. Be merciful in the presence of mercilessness -- most attempt to get even. Have compassion in the presence of anger -- for anger is merely fear. Illuminate your world with your heart without hesitation --

-- for love is the thing over which nothing has dominion.

DAY 44
ENCOURAGEMENT

Encouragement can make all the difference in a person's life path, even one kind sentence truly meant from the heart. Should we ever become "too busy" to reach out with one sentence, or one text, or a one-lined email, then that imbalance is within us. If we are receiving encouragement from others yet do not pass it on when we see another in need, that encouragement energy directed toward us will stop, as we create an imbalance. Take the few seconds to pass on beautiful words to another who you may clearly see needs a lift. Take the time to value someone's contributions. Take the time to make HUMAN your journey. It may only be ten seconds out of your day, but could turn another person's world around forever, and ignite within them a feeling of purpose and belonging.

You never know when that person needing a lift will be you.

DAY 45
FREEDOM

We spend our days fretting, doubting, betraying, resenting, longing, hiding, hurting, and coveting. We spend our nights fearing, plotting, yearning, and regretting. We live the lie of Not Enough -- money, toys, partners, homes, things, opportunities, recognition, acceptance. And then we claim we don't have enough hours in the day. What would we do with all our free time if our day and night consisted of simply being grateful? It is the awe-inspiring responsibility of our freedom, not the predictable imprisonment of our misery --

-- that we fear the most.

DAY 46
COUNT YOUR BLESSINGS

Though experiencing disappointment is part of being alive, gratitude seems to be in short demand when we experience fear. However, it is being able to experience gratitude that allows us to count our blessings in spite of the emotional or situational "hail storm" we may be enduring. To "look on the bright side" is not an escapist behavior. It is enacting and igniting the principles of Spiritual Physics -- Likes Attracts Like -- drawing to us that which we truly desire. In the midst of a hail storm, note something that's NOT broken in that moment -- and for that, give thanks. Allowing ourselves to experience gratitude for what IS working in our lives then allows us not only to hug the Universe, but others, for what we've received -- and for the blessings bestowed upon us. Gratitude is the Gift of Acceptance that only we can give to ourselves. Hold in gratitude all that IS working, and all that is good -- in your life.

And watch more "working" situations appear!

DAY 47
WHAT IS HEARTBREAK

The spiritual physics of Heart Break: What we call "heartbreak" is actually "soul break". The heart chakra, which sits mid chest, energetically interprets the soul's "break" in connection to another person. Our physical body is hard-wired to our chakra system, thus the physical sensation of our "heart breaking" when our soul is separated from a loved one's energy. Upon the "un-entwining" of our soul from another person's energy field, we experience a dramatic drop in physical energy which was provided by the connection to the other person. Our bodies will take time to re-establish a singular (non-shared) flow of chi through our chakra system. This re-establishment period is commonly called "the blues", where we can't get up out of bed or off the couch, accompanied by flu-like lethargy due to our bodies adjusting to half the yield of daily energy. "Dying of a broken heart" is actually the process of one's chakra and electrical system failing to make the adjustment back to a non- shared chi pattern. As a result, the physical organs which rely on our electrical system -- the heart and brain -- shut down.

Though rare, this phenomenon occurs between souls with heavily-tied past life and / or karmic connections.

DAY 48
CHANGE

The many changes in life that we face are not nearly as daunting as the moment we realize that the energy we refer to as "change" is actually the constant -- not the transition. Make friends with Change. She's actually a pretty exciting pal to have around --

-- and she's here to help you.

DAY 49
SHINE

There is nothing you can't do when you allow your light to shine brightly! Today -- SHINE!

And let others shield their eyes if they must.

DAY 50
THE BIG PICTURE

We are purposefully made to each see the world through a unique lens. By comparing these views, we create a vastly different "picture" of life. Though you may be observing the same view as someone standing right next to you, your neighbor's "snapshot" of life contains a completely different angle. It is only through continuing to examine the "perspective collage" that we are then able to see the depth of what is truly in front of us. Don't be afraid to compare notes with those whose perceptions differ from yours.

We're all an intricate part of decoding and interpreting the "big picture".

DAY 51
QUIET TIME

The Universe whispers to us in the Quiet Spaces within our lives. If we never leave a blank moment in our day, we do not leave room to hear the Utterance from the Heavens. God is a warm whisper not a shout. It's not God's job to slow us down enough to pay attention. It's our job to pay attention when we slow down.

"Quiet Time" is never really quiet, if you relax -- and listen.

DAY 52
FAITH

    Insecurity is a symptom of a loss in faith, whether in a person, a system, or most often, a lack of faith in our perceived worth to others -- and ourselves. Succumbing to insecurity is much like drowning: We thrash against our own current until we've exhausting ourselves in our own depths only to achieve our greatest fear -- sinking silently into our own abyss -- the murky place within us we fear the most. When finding yourself drowning in insecurity -- stop thrashing. Be still. Float above the issue that is enticing you to struggle. Separate yourself from the pull of the frantic current below and realize -- you can trust yourself not to engage the flurry of the storm passing through your mind.

    Faith is belief when belief has lost its compass.

DAY 53
WHAT'S TRYING TO HAPPEN

No matter what it looks like on paper today, no matter what is hitting the fan today, greet today with gratitude and elation as if it were arriving on your doorstep with your dream job, dream life, and all the resolution and prosperity you are able to handle. Why? Because no matter what distraction may hold your thoughts, that distraction is only temporary. The truth is that today is providing one more brick toward finishing the foundation of your spirit. Right now, at this very minute, though you may not be aware -- construction is underway on your most astounding life path possible. Maybe that's why it's so loud in your world lately? Construction is a messy process. However, rest in true knowledge that God / Universe has it handled in ways we don't even know exist even when the pieces on the game board have been spilled onto the floor. Your day belongs to you today. You only get to use it once. Commit to joy today, make a decision not to let the turkeys get you down, and stand back in awe to watch The Design take shape.

It's amazing what happens once we let happen what's been trying to happen all along.

DAY 54
SPIRITUAL DIET

The Spiritual Food Chain has an apex predator: Fear. When we succumb to fear, we often feed the pain that is fueling it. As we ingest the fear that dines solely on pain, the result is the uncontrollable regurgitation of our own dignity. Feeling pain is part of being alive.

Feeding on pain is an unhealthy choice in spiritual diet.

DAY 55
TRUE STRENGTH

True strength is not found through force, nor sharp words, nor wealth, but in the uncertain space between action --

-- where one's endurance is motivated by the needs of others.

DAY 56
MIRROR EFFECT

Be exactly what it is you'd like to see in others. You're searching for those qualities in yourself. If you wish people to be more polite -- then enact more kindness. If you wish people to be more understanding -- enact more honed listening skills. If you wish people to be more helpful -- enact greater assistance toward others.

It is in this "mirror effect" that we find our greatest qualities within by outwardly taking action.

DAY 57
YOUR CALLING

Every soul is born with a calling. Sometimes, the trials of daily life shout louder than the design of our destiny. Listen for the whisper of the calling within you, because destiny is created, not bestowed. We must co-create with the Universe the path for our calling to thrive, and first, we must acknowledge that pull on our soul. Do not fret over "how" your calling will be made manifest. That is the job of The Universe. Our job is to accept our calling, consciously, and take one small step toward it, in this three dimensional reality. No step is too small as long as it is taken. The rest will tumble into our path for us to arrange along our way.

Listen. Your calling is calling *you*.

DAY 58
YOUR DESIGN

Our spirit is timeless. We are the sum total of everything we have said and done and everything we hope to say and do -- all at once. "Day to day" only exists on our schedules and calendars. Yet in spite of that wide parameter, we still worry that we don't possess what we need to emotionally and spiritually provide for ourselves. We possess far greater gifts internally than our ability to comprehend our own potential externally. When we are incapable of grasping this, our friends, family, and even foes, will remind us of our true strengths. You are infinitely capable, created in the image of Creator God -- who is infinitely capable.

Take solace and rest in your design.

DAY 59
DIS-EASE

Hatred is a disease of the mind. Greed is a disease of the body. Apathy is a disease of the spirit. When Mind-Body-Spirit is in DIS-ease, one can CHOOSE ease by applying cures that are created by the heart: Forgiveness for Hatred, Acceptance for Greed, and Empathy for Apathy.

Forgiveness, Acceptance, and Empathy: the Triple Threat against Darkness.

DAY 60
SPIRITUAL BINGING

"Eating spiritual junk food" is the worst kind of binging. We crave connection so we "hook up" for a night then feel awkward the next day. We crave being heard so we start an argument then must live with ugly words that all have experienced. We crave validation so we push our opinions on others until we are unbearable. We crave having purpose so we try and assert ourselves where we are not needed and suffer rejection. That which does not feed our soul instead packs "extra pounds" onto our psyche -- something we have to work much harder to "take off" later. Instead of spiritually binging when suffering under a spiritual craving, ask the three key questions: "What is it I truly desire right now? Though I feel a need, do I feel desperate at this moment? Would I do anything to satisfy the craving?" If the answer is yes, then we are not "hungry" for something to fill a need but panicked that nothing will fill us. The latter cannot be quenched by anything we "ingest" --

-- but only through discontinuing our relationship with the illusion of limitation.

DAY 61
TODAY VS TOMORROW

We seek knowledge of the future to assist us in sculpting today's choices. However, today's choices build tomorrow's future. Instead, embrace today for all that it is, and immerse yourself in activity. This will create the momentum needed to bring in the change you seek. An object in motion stays in motion. An object at rest stays at rest.

It's "Physics", not "Psychic".

DAY 62
PERCEPTION

Remember: Sometimes, what you think is "going on" -- isn't. In an upsetting situation, always take a deep breath, then respond --

-- rather than react.

DAY 63
CHOOSE

Step away from ugliness. Set aside anger. Our world encourages deception, blaming -- all tools of the Dark wielded by those in pain against others to cause pain. Illusion provides no true shelter from our karmic path. It only buys us time before the consequences of our actions catch up with us. Pray for the spirits of those in our world who have fallen prey to their own illusion. Theirs is a frightening heartbreak once the karmic lesson is delivered. Choose a path of peace. Choose truth. Choose integrity.

In these three things one finds deliverance from chaos.

DAY 64
LOVE

Love is the strength. Love is the courage. Love is the invitation. Love is the language. Love is the balm. Love is the shelter. Love is the understanding. Love is the question. And love is the answer. Send LOVE before you and walls crumble. Leave LOVE behind you and scorched fields will yield a bounty. Bring LOVE with you and ignite hope. Be LOVE and others learn to love. ACCEPT love -- and others learn the value in connection. GIVE love because it's what you're designed to do. Love isn't about outcome. It's a state of being. To love is to connect to all Creation.

To love is to share the heartbeat of God, if only for a moment.

DAY 65
LIKE ATTRACTS LIKE

Life is an interesting contrary experience. The actions of individuals, toward others, do not always match how they wish to be treated. We are able to witness our value in another's life by how others choose to treat us in our greatest moments of need. Anyone can shine with no expectations placed upon them, becoming the "store-shelf hero" in the moment. It is true strength, character, and commitment that rises to the occasion for another when *the other* is in need -- not simply when it is convenient for us. What we put in, we get back. We are clearly seen for who and what we are as observed by our actions -- not how we wish others would perceive us to be, on paper, on record, or as per our history. Many will be inconvenienced, even indignant, as the people they have counted on, to "patch" leaks in their personhood, life, or schedule, shall disappear in response to inequity. This is the transcendence of consciousness in action. Reciprocators will find one other and what they shall build will be unbreakable. Takers will grapple for a shrinking pool of those who will fit into their agenda, constantly re-stocking the shelves as those they burn through find their value elsewhere. As humanity is ignited with personal relevance, many will abandon situations that treat the individual's relevance with apathy. Business and personal relationships could not be more polarized nor more simple to navigate:

Do you feel "owed" a debt by life and those around you, or do you feel you owe life because you are in its debt?

DAY 66
KINDNESS

Help clean up the ethers and try something different today: Whoever you come into contact with, even a total stranger, make yourself pay them a compliment. Just pick out something that catches your eye and make a positive comment, clear out of the blue. The Spiritual Physics of Kindness not only affect the person you're speaking with but affect you, too --

-- as well as leaving GREAT energy behind in your surroundings.

DAY 67
OBSERVATION

We overlook the most brilliant and perfect gifts bestowed to us by The Universe in our quest to create our version of those very same gifts. Often when we are given something for free -- when something falls "in our lap" -- we do not recognize its value. Not until we labor rigorously to achieve half the free gift do we assign value to what we've been given. Be mindful not to take for granted the gifts freely given to the spirit while the ego creates twice as much work for half the yield.

We don't need to be the author for the novel to be brilliant.

DAY 68
REACH OUT

    Conquering then crossing the border of our own comfort zone is a strategic win in the soul's turf war against our Greatest Fears. When given the choice, always reach out to people. You never know which stranger in your life is actually your new dearest friend --

-- yet undiscovered.

DAY 69
FOCUS

Remaining focused isn't a discipline.

It's a choice.

DAY 70
PATIENCE

When we find ourselves lashing out at another, when we find inside of ourselves a buried fuse that is smoldering toward a powder keg of unrest, that is the time to extend patience toward the situation which exposed the secret store of munitions we've packed within our soul -- of which we may have been unaware. We can't disarm a bomb we never knew existed. If not located, that same deeply hidden cavern of explosives can be triggered without our knowledge, taking out not only the person who unknowingly tripped the wire, but everything else inside of us -- all of our foundations and bridges, in an instant. We are then left trapped beneath our own rubble, stranded on the island inside of ourselves --

-- a victim of our own internal terrorist attack.

DAY 71
CLAIMS

It is that after which we strive that we, too, must struggle. The person who claims great riches fears poverty. The person who claims great courage wrestles back cowardice. The person who claims great strength is not strong.

It is the person who lays claim to nothing, yet acts on behalf of everything, who is rich in courageous strength.

DAY 72
REFRAMING DISAPPOINTMENT

Sometimes, experiencing disappointment acts as a way to point out what truly holds value to us. We can only be disappointed if we have emotional investment in a situation.

Emotional investment is the reaching vine that grows out of Hope.

DAY 73
IN THE NOW

Our goals, dreams, and aspirations do not amount to much if our daily life activities are lacking support for them. Without tightening up our actions in the now, we push our future plans even further into the future. Like attempting to retrieve a basketball out of swimming pool with a broomstick, soon our target is out of reach all together. Our future is nothing more than the cumulative actions of TODAY. If we want our future to arrive "faster" -- we must change our activities in the MOMENT.

We cannot have one outcome without the other.

DAY 74
TIMING

When it's time for us to go forward in our lives, we simply GO and it is effortless -- retrograde or no retrograde, isms or no isms. When Life decides it's time for us to step onto our "next phase", there is absolutely nothing that can stop that forward momentum. Nothing. When it is time -- the very ground beneath our feet will move to get us wherever we need to be.

We become a moving miracle.

DAY 75
BURNING BRIDGES

Forgiveness is a choice so "bridge burning" is a bit extreme. There are certain energy signatures, people, places, and situations that no longer serve our path, nor do we serve theirs. Our lack of participation with those signatures can be equal parts gentle and firm without the unnecessary "bridge burning" drama. In fact, our lack of further participation is often a key piece of someone else's learning process, as well as our own. Letting go of the responsibility to "heal" a situation, individual, or path that is either not ours to heal, or is beyond our capacity to affect change, is key in all parties moving forward. I call this action "releasing bridges". That way, someone else may find active use for the passageway that once brought us from point A to point B. May we bless, not burn, the bridges that brought us to where we are today, even if we choose to never travel them again.

After all -- they did, at one time, faithfully bear our full weight.

DAY 76
CONNECTING

Remember to reach out even when you don't want to. It's during those times that we just "don't want to deal with anyone" that truly --

-- we need others the most.

DAY 77
PROVISION

When it comes to worrying about money or provision -- never lose track of the basics. Prosperity is like electricity running through the walls: You can plug the same lamp into 8 outlets all around the room, and no matter what outlet, it will always light up. Our prosperity is not limited to one "outlet". We live our lives unaware of how much electricity is running through our walls.

So are we often unaware of the unlimited bounty all around us.

DAY 78
CONNECTING

People rarely stop you to tell you that you are amazing. Yet they'll go out of their way to tell ten people about what they perceive your shortcomings to be. This doesn't mean that ten people now know your "faults". It means that ten people now know the weakness of one very insecure person. Instead of spreading what we don't like about others, try spreading what you DO like.

Like attracts Like in Spiritual Physics.

DAY 79
DEFINITION OF GRACE

None of us, no matter how centered, connected, or enlightened, are exempt from having a "moment". Jesus the Christ was so upset at a fig tree for not bearing fruit when he was hungry that his disdain killed it. The point of this life is not to *never* rock the apple cart, or misstep, or misperceive, or make a mistake. The point is how we handle all of the above afterwards. We execute behaviors that at times we cannot control in the moment because we require the clarity brought on afterwards -- a clarity life has been attempting to bring to us in other ways. By extending others grace -- room to "be human" -- we extend this permission to ourselves. Own what is yours to apologize for and grant others compassion in their apologies. This does not make you weak. It makes you the bending reed within the wind storm --

-- while others are snapped low at the stalk.

DAY 80
YOUR FLAVOR

Each one of us is an important ingredient within the delicate recipe of human consciousness. Our part makes a difference in the flavor, whether a teaspoon or a cup full. We are designed to blend well with one another.

Just like the perfect Thanksgiving Turkey, we taste best after a little heat has been applied.

DAY 81
REGENERATION

We resist allowing that which no longer serves us -- jobs, addictions to dramas, certain relationships -- to simply fall away. We attempt to hug them tightly to us because they are part of our past that has helped define who we are up to that point. In essence, it is often not the worn out job, the worn out dramas, or the worn out relationships that we are fearful of losing. Instead, it is the loss of who we feel we are without them. Even our skin sloughs off the top layer of dead cells so the new may grow up beneath. If our skin refused to release the exhausted cells that have served their purpose, how monstrously distorted would our face become in the mirror? Like our skin, our soul never stops growing.

To cling to the exhausted parts of our life path is to deform our spirit.

DAY 82
RECEIVING LOVE

Allowing yourself to be loved is as important as loving others. To receive love, we must open our emotional gate and expose who we truly are. While the gate is opened, there is a risk that others may see our unkempt mess behind the curtain.

Yet it is in trusting others to accept our imperfections when love is truly experienced.

DAY 83
BE BRAVE

Be brave. Anyone can appear the hero when the spotlight burns hot.

But it takes true courage to remain steadfast when no one but fear is watching.

DAY 84
HANG IN THERE

Hang in there. You're worth it. Nothing is as bad as it feels like it is in the moment it's imploding. Don't live in the worst-case-scenario you're designing for your future and don't dwell in the mistakes of the past. Neither actually exist. The only thing that TRULY exists -- is you, reading this -- right now. Feel yourself breathe.

You can do this.

DAY 85
CREATE PEACE

Aspire. Inspire. Reach deep. Reach out. Be a stepping stone. Not a stumbling block. Avoid chaos. Invite growth. Release expectations. Replace them with wonderment. Allow others to be who they truly are. Bless them. Allow yourself to be who you truly are. Bless you. Above all things -- create peace, which disarms and heals. Peace comes from within you. It's highly contagious.

May you start an epidemic of global proportion.

DAY 86
YOU'RE WORTHY

The greatest gifts in your life are what come to you when you aren't looking. We believe we know what we truly want until what we truly need is presented to us. That's the way Spirit works. When life gives you a gift, rip off the paper and say thank you. Universe knows what its doing when it comes to timing even if we don't get it. Tucking the gift away until later is like opening all the presents from your 8th birthday party on your 16th instead: That mutant ninja turtle somehow loses its relevance. Embrace the gifts you don't expect. They're called surprises. Practice believing you're worthy enough to receive.

Then watch your life change.

DAY 87
MIRACLES

When something that seems impossible stands before you, remember that Miracles would not be Miracles if the odds were never stacked against you. Give the Universe a chance to be extraordinary today.

BELIEVE!

DAY 88
EMBRACE CONNECTION

To embrace our ability to connect to one another is to become the strongest we'll ever be. The Golden Gate Bridge is able to be suspended thanks to thousands of tiny cables within the big "tubes" that string from one end of the bridge to the other. Each tiny cable bears part of the weight of the bridge. As we connect to others in our life, each person bears part of the weight of our journey, as do we for those who connect to us. Don't fear forging deep connections in your life.

They are the cable system that keeps the spirit suspended over turbulent waters below.

DAY 89
GROWTH REQUIRES COURAGE

Without risk, the human sense of accomplishment would not exist. That which challenges us to overcome also gifts us with growth. Growth requires courage. Allow buried emotions to surface in order to release them --

-- as trapped birds back into the wild.

DAY 90
DO WHAT YOU CAN

Don't be afraid to do even a little, if a little is all you have to give. Through the most extraordinary of times --

-- even the most understated of acts can make the most difference.

DAY 91
CHALLENGE YOURSELF

Today, challenge yourself to accomplish something you aren't sure you can even do, be it physical, mental, emotional -- you name it. You'll be both shocked and amazed at your ability to overcome what you believed were your own limitations. Challenge yourself.

Allow the Universe the opportunity to provide you with experiencing the miracle of your own capabilities and potential.

DAY 92
EXPLORE ALL POSSIBILITIES

Reaching past our usual "comfort zone" is a wonderful way to make new friends, learn new skills, explore new food, try new clothes, take a more scenic route, discover new music, realize something different about our spiritual understanding, and sample all possibilities in general. Every day we are given the opportunity to explore an entirely new Universe by simply making a new choice. What are you waiting for? Life is a temporary theme park. Enjoy as many of the rides as possible.

You've already paid your admission.

DAY 93
SHARE LOVE

It doesn't have to be fancy, or deep, or worded like a guru -- just telling someone you love them, and meaning it, is the single most powerful healing tool on the planet. Begin healing the planet from under your own roof, right now.

Start with the hearts that depend on you.

DAY 94
FEELINGS AREN'T FENCES

It's okay to be afraid. It's okay to feel abandoned. It's okay to feel as though the path has dead-ended. Yet recognize all those emotions for what they are: Feelings, not Fences. A feeling is not a concrete thing. It's a reflection of how we are viewing our situation, right at that moment -- a snapshot of our perspective, frozen in an emotion. Just as a single photo taken at a party does not trap one's entire life in the camera, experiencing a disheartening feeling does not freeze one's entire life in that moment. Take a deep breath and let it pass. And just like the morning after a party when the photos are reviewed --

-- this, too, shall be nothing but a blurry memory where *why* the photo was taken cannot even be recalled.

DAY 95
THE NEXT STEP

Do not mourn the loss of the energy that has stopped desiring your participation as it does not mourn the loss of you. Instead, find gratitude in what you have gained and invite your next greatest adventure of spirit, mind, heart, and body into your life. The Universe does not throw any of us away, though our fear attempts to convince us we are "disposable". This is a lie of the Dark, designed to defeat us on the precipice of our next most important transition:

The change that delivers us the life we've always desired.

DAY 96
OBSTACLES ARE INSPIRATIONS

In the face of what appears a monumental task, remember: The cycle of life is propelled by repeatedly overcoming "never-been-encountered" obstacles. We are made to problem solve and overcome. We are Children of Creation -- we are one with endless possibility and endless Creative potential. We once perceived the path that dead-ended into a cliff wall as "the end" of our walk -- until someone invented the ladder. Obstacles are simply Inspirations.

Be INSPIRED in your day today!

DAY 97
NO SEPARATION

There is nothing that we can say or do that will separate us from the love of our Universal Parent Creator/God. However, we are each free to choose the illusion of separation from The Source. This "choice" defines our reality, though in reality -- nothing has changed.

An apple is still an apple, even if we call it an orange.

DAY 98
FEET

Sometimes the hardest path to stay focused on is the path whose dirt is right beneath our feet.

Where are your feet today?

DAY 99
SYNCHRONICITY

All living beings require a primary connection to something else in order to thrive. A barnacle requires a rock. A king crab requires a biomass. Cells require other cells. Angelic life requires pure love (God Source). Human Beings require a connection to their own relevance via a third party, in order to thrive: A spouse, a career, children, parents, family -- you name it. The biggest miscommunication occurs when one person's "need" for relevance does not match another's while on a life path together, and feelings get hurt. Instead, if we were able to be honest with one another about what truly fueled our feeling of relevance in life, instead of trying to shift our needs to something they are not to make others comfortable (thus causing resentment toward the other person, among many other things), we would be able to not only honor our own design, but that of others, without feeling like we "haven't gotten ours" from that person. Only we can be honest with ourselves about what we feel our "rock" in life truly is -- our anchor, our point of relevance. And just as we should not judge others in what their "rock" is -- we should not judge ourselves. The skill is in aligning our life relevance with others'.

Therein lies synchronicity in purpose, path, and heart.

DAY 100
MAGNETISM

Be exactly who you are. There are all sorts of ideas about "who we need to be" in business and in relationships that are simply untrue. Certainly there is needing to be professional and needing to be courteous. However, being someone that you are not to earn the favor of others will then place you in the position to be deceived by others who are attempting to earn favors from you. Like Attracts Like in Spiritual Physics. Opposite resonations repel one another. Be exactly WHAT you are, and WHAT you seek shall find you.

It is the magnetism of the Universe.

DAY 101
EMBRACE LOVE

Embrace love. It comes in many forms and feeds many aspects of our soul. It is timeless, bodiless, and is free to both give and receive. It is the breath of God, the bond between us, the fulcrum of forgiveness, the flint of passion, the language of selflessness, and the seed of peace. Embrace love not as something you seek but as who you are.

Now watch your world change.

DAY 102
STAND STILL

When we find ourselves struggling to be part of something, whether it's a relationship, a job, a social set, or just a general life path – that's when it's time to take a few steps back and recognize that perhaps what we're struggling after does not need --or want-- our participation. Sometimes, the things that we think we need the most – aren't what we need at all. If they were what we required for our highest growth and the growth of others around us, the Universe would help us along. Sometimes, what we truly require is nothing more than simply standing still: standing in our own peace, to try and unearth in ourselves that which we have hidden from ourselves...our map to everything that brings us joy, even if we are yet to understand what that joy truly is at this juncture of our journey. The only instruction we truly require from the Universe –

-- is how to remain patient.

DAY 103
BAD RECYCLING

Your pain and hurt is valid. Yet don't use your hurt to hurt others.

That's the only kind of recycling that ruins the environment.

DAY 104
YOUR RELEVANCE

Always have faith that you are here, on this planet, for a *reason*. You may not know what that reason yet is, and there may be more than one reason. But you are much, much more to The Universe than simply something that takes up space.

You are a mission of great importance.

DAY 105
BELIEVING FEAR

The mind is powerful and defines our "reality". Be mindful to pay attention to what *is* going on, not what you *fear* is going on. Don't wage battles toward a situation that isn't actually happening.

You'll never land one punch, fighting an adversary that only exists in your head.

DAY 106
BUILDING YOUR PATH

Don't be afraid to roll up your sleeves and get your hands dirty -- in your own life. Many times, our life, just like an old home, needs a periodic overhaul. EVERYTHING in this third dimension falls into disrepair eventually. It doesn't mean you didn't build it well enough the first time. It means something greater is attempting to replace it. So have JOY in putting on your grubby clothes and gutting out the "old" in your life to make way for the "new". Clean the emotional mold out from beneath the cupboards. Shine up the life path windows so you can truly see the view. Build a new addition onto the "house" of the soul.

We are the happiest when the dirt beneath our fingernails comes from working our own life path.

DAY 107
DON'T MISTAKE THE PAUSE

During the times in our lives where we feel incredibly stagnant -- like everything we ever worked for is going nowhere -- don't mistake the pause in your forward momentum for "the end". What we view as "stagnation" is the Universe's moment to "Lock and Load" before you blast through that glass ceiling. Just like a jetliner on the runway, the pause in your forward movement is your cue to tighten your seatbelt low and tight across your lap --

-- because it's time for take off!

DAY 108
DOUBT

You are not weak for experiencing Doubt, but in experiencing Doubt you are seeking great illumination. Doubt is the inspiration for truth, and truth is the inspiration for discovery.

Without discovery, we are but meat and bones, biding our time until breath wears us out.

DAY 109
EVERYTHING CHANGES

Everything changes. We change. You're not the same as you were ten years ago. Not even five. Not even three. So let go. Not give up. Just let go. There's a difference. Giving Up means that you admit life does not hold any more opportunity for you. Letting Go means you admit that life has much more in store for you, and you must make room. So make room. It's okay. Everything changes. Even you.

You're supposed to.

DAY 110
TODAY'S MANTRA

Mantra for Today: I am just right the way that I am designed. I am not expected to handle "it all" -- only that which is set before me. I am not responsible for managing the perceptions and reactions of others.

I am only responsible for how I choose to perceive and respond.

DAY 111
EFFECT TO CAUSE

Resist the urge to blame those "in charge" for your lack of "taking charge" of those tasks which are yours to enact. We often find discontent with others, claiming they fall short in serving us, when it is we who fall drastically short of not only serving ourselves -- but serving others. If you find you harbor feelings of fault or abandonment toward another, ask yourself: What have I not done for myself today that would provide a sense of accomplishment and safety in my life? Only YOU can reassure yourself that you are capable of taking care of yourself. Though input from others may provide support, it is our job -- not that of our boss, our spouse, or the Universe -- to pick ourselves up and keep moving. If you crave change -- then change.

The rest is "the effect" to your "cause".

DAY 112
IT'S NOT ABOUT WINNING

Following your heart is one thing. Acting on what your heart is compelling you to do is another. Courage is the process of *doing* in spite of what you're *feeling*. Where there is great hesitation, there is great opportunity for growth. Before you stop permanently with your toes parked on life's starting line, remember: It's not about winning the race. It's about getting off the blocks.

An object in motion stays in motion.

DAY 113
REDESIGN

Where there is great upheaval, there is great opportunity for redesign. Where there is opportunity for redesign, there is opportunity for re-evaluation. In our moments of need, we often hear "You know I'm always here for you", or "Let me know if there's anything I can do". Yet more often than not when we reach out, the line then goes dead. Anyone can be a great friend to us when we are strong, amazing, the life of the party, standing in the gap for others' needs, picking up the tab, providing professional assistance, being the shoulder to cry on, and asking nothing of anyone. The mark of true dedication of another in our lives, or the mark of our true dedication to others, is our ability to make room for those we care about even when it isn't convenient for us -- and when we gain nothing at all except the satisfaction that we aided in healing someone's soul in their moment of need. Attempting to "schedule in" assisting someone through their crisis moment to a time that's more convenient for us is like attempting to place a saddle on a bullet after it's been shot:

No one gets anywhere and somebody always ends up with a hole in their heart.

DAY 114
IN CHARGE

Our dreams and aspirations are the soul's way of reminding the doubting conscious mind--

-- that it was never in charge.

DAY 115
HANG ON

Don't give up! Whatever you're going through -- don't give up. Darkness uses the illusion of isolation, desolation, and hopelessness to encourage us to "let go" when we're hanging from an emotional cliff. But don't let go. You're only moments away from being pulled up by The Light into the life that's meant for YOU.

Hang on!

DAY 116
NAVIGATION

When everything collapses around you and the footing beneath you crumbles, the heart panics. It is in these moments of confusion, loss and despair that we feel the Illusion of Separation the most, plunged into the dark of our own deepest fears. The challenge in these moments is to not attempt to "overcome" the feeling consuming us, as the struggle against the churning and painful current will deplete what small emotional resources we do have left. The challenge is to relax into the current, floating atop the river outstretched in the sun, calmed by the faith that wherever the river is headed, it's had one million years to carve its journey along the way --

-- and perhaps it knows where it's going.

DAY 117
MAKE YOUR PEACE

Find the peace within yourself that you wish someone or something else would provide. Once you achieve this feat --

-- fear has no where within you to reside.

DAY 118
THE CHOICE

Energetically, we reap what we sow in this lifetime. This is not to say that bad things don't happen to good people because they do. Yet overall, our experience on this planet is exactly what we choose to make it: Danger is real -- Fear is a choice. Pain is real -- Suffering is a choice. Sadness is real -- Devastation is a choice. Loneliness is real -- Isolation is a choice. Anger is real -- Forgiveness is a choice. Love is real -- Hope is a choice.

Ask yourself today not how life chooses to experience you, but how you choose to experience life.

DAY 119
GRIEF

Grief is a layered emotion, one that can't easily be scraped from the bottom of the soul's shoe. When working through grief, be kind to yourself. Grief takes as long as it takes to work its way up through the crevices of your consciousness. It is a process much like a sliver being slowly expelled from the body -- the spirit eventually ejects the root cause of the grief, over time. So come out of judgment with yourself and relax into the process.

Grief is a deep cleaning of the psyche and a time-release capsule swallowed by the heart.

DAY 120
EVOLVE

People push away what it is they want the most: Jobs, people, opportunities, places to live, etc. At this evolutionary space in human development, this goes beyond "self-defeating behavior". This is soul-defeating behavior. When we create justifications of "protecting" our hearts, head, lives, etc., by pushing away or denying ourselves what is calling to us in a healthy way, we become our own karma. It does not protect us to deny that which is screaming to us along our path to engage. Instead, it exhausts our energies to ignore the prompt or call. If you know you've been resisting a big change, or burying a big recognition within yourself, remind yourself that all forward-progressing life on Earth has continued to evolve. Refusing to evolve in the way the Universe has designed for your highest good is certainly an option.

Yet all things that don't evolve -- die out.

DAY 121
LOSE THE SELF

Be not dissuaded from your path by ugliness. We are living in a real world attempting to be made false by those who fear the unpredictability of the human spirit. Yet the human spirit, born from Light, cannot be caged. Seek not your relevance in the world. Instead, seek your relevance TO the world, and all paths will be cleared to meet your true purpose -- even if that purpose remains yet unknown.

We must lose "the self" to find ourselves.

DAY 122
WITH PURPOSE

Today's mantra: I don't require an identity in order to matter. Who I am is more than enough.

I am designed on purpose, with purpose.

DAY 123
UNPLUG

Sometimes you have to just "be". It's not fancy and it doesn't win any awards. Just "being" doesn't fulfill any agendas, doesn't cross anything off any lists, and changes no one's life -- but yours. It's not about learning a lesson or working out karma. It's not about anything. That's the point. Unplug for a day. The world will go on. Your job will survive. True friends will live without an immediate text back. We become addicted to a false sense of relevance in our lives and forget where our true peace originates. It is within this peace that our most pure and free identity resides. Though we all have responsibilities, we neglect to remember we've chosen most of them. Just be. For one day. Without judging yourself for doing so. If you unplug for a day and truly believe your world will end --

-- that problem does not lie with the world.

DAY 124
PERCEIVED NEEDS

There are certain things in life that we "think we need" in order to validate our careers, our lives, or our relationships. However, the moment we let go of these preconceived "needs", we've validated our careers, our lives and our relationships by acknowledging their worth in our present. To wait on "needs" is to continually seek validation from the future, which can't ever exist because we won't validate today.

And only today builds our tomorrow.

DAY 125
FAITH

Free-falling into "Faith" isn't "Free" at all. It takes great effort to let go and great patience with ourselves during the process. When we're faced with uncertainty, it requires focus to tune out fear-based "worse-case scenarios" of the future -- and replace them with the beautiful gifts actually occurring in the moment. It takes dedication to bypass knee-jerk behaviors driven by desperation -- and replace them with the action of peaceful observation. Once we learn how to unlearn years worth of band-aid "panic emotionality" -- once we make the decision to let go of an old belief system where our Low Ego requires us to REACT, not RESPOND -- we are then able to experience the greatest spiritual and emotional freedom of all: Faith. Faith is the act of accepting that even though we can't get it handled -- Someone Else can. There is no such thing as "blind faith". Faith is a choice, then a discipline, then a new way of life.

Today, work toward enacting the energy of Faith in your life -- so tomorrow you don't have to.

DAY 126
NOTE FOR YOU

    I'm not here to make you believe in anything. I'm just here. I do, however, believe in you.

-- God

DAY 127
RISK

Life is woven from risk. Without risk, we do not experience growth or a sense of achievement. Without risk, we stay inside the box and stagnate. Sometimes we risk and experience loss. Yet we always learn, so we gain. We risk everyday -- sharing our deepest truths and hoping those truths don't become bludgeoning tools; opening our hearts when our heads want to slam the safety valve closed; giving of our last dollar because we know provision is around the corner. To "risk" means also to walk on faith -- or to gamble -- that the Universe has the house odds stacked in your favor. If you've risked and lost, it was not taking the risk that was the issue. Risk is an exhilarating teacher once we stop demonizing it's design. Risk is the wind in the sails of invention, the springboard into entrepreneurial endeavors, the ring on the finger of finances everywhere, the college diploma in the hand of the 40-something, and the "x" in Extreme Sports. If you don't have any idea about the outcome yet you take a step, you're not "taking a risk".

You're living life.

DAY 128
YOU'RE TOUGHER THAN YOU THINK

There is nothing that you cannot face down in this lifetime. You are built to overcome, designed by Greatness, for greatness. You are made by Creation, to create. Your perspective is valuable and your contribution to this lifetime is greater than you'll ever realize. When we stop deciding that we are "not enough", what we truly *are* begins to shine, lighting our path --

-- and the path of others in need.

DAY 129
ANGLE OF THE LIGHT

As you stand in the doorway of transition, be not frightened by the shadow of change cast upon your feet. Remember that the angle of The Light determines the shadow's length -- not the size of the change ahead. Light shining overhead, out of reach, casts a small shadow on the ground. Light shining directly in front of us to illuminate our path then casts a lengthy shadow. If you are witnessing a long shadow of change cast into your doorway, then know The Light has gone before you, a lantern in the darkness --

-- to prepare your way.

DAY 130
THE GREATEST LIE

Always allow the Universe to take you where your gifts and talents would be best utilized. The greatest wisdom is in knowing that our plan isn't always the best plan Always tell those you love that you love them. The greatest strength is in the vulnerability of the soul. Never fear anything.

The greatest lie is that we are incapable.

DAY 131
FLOAT TRIP

Only by charging across waters too murky to avoid the snags can you truly appreciate floating atop the river, letting the current set your course.

Today, enjoy the float trip.

DAY 132
BLOCKING THE DOOR JAM

When doors are slamming closed around you, don't be afraid to let them. We often spend far too much time throwing ourselves in the door jam to keep the passageway open, and in the meantime, we become pretty beat-up in the process. We block the door jam for a number of reasons, but most often, we'd rather be crushed in a familiar old doorway than freely walk through an unknown hallway. Allow the old doors to close, fully. The passageway has served its purpose, bringing you to the next portal in your journey. Have faith that the doorway now opening in front of you is open not simply for "a" reason, but for THE reason: You. Are you ready boots?

Start walkin'!

DAY 133
HELD HOSTAGE

Allowing our fears to make decisions for our life path is like allowing a terrorist to make decisions on behalf of hostages.

Either way, all are held captive.

DAY 134
NOT RESPONSIBLE

In order to become the person that you truly are, you must stop acting like the person you are not. You can only be who you are. That will either work for people or it won't. The good news is --

-- you're not responsible for the "won't".

DAY 135
MOMENTUM

The best motivator in the world is momentum. An object in motion stays in motion. Keep moving forward, one foot in front of the other. When the direction is unclear (and the path just may become muddier before it's all said and done) simply keep moving. Movement is 9/10ths of successful change. The other 1/10th is conviction. However, conviction without movement is how our incarceration system works: A convict is detained. Don't be locked within the Prison of Indecision.

Always move forward, if only an inch at a time.

DAY 136
IMPERVIOUS

If we align with our feelings instead of our fears, we are able to respond, rather than react, to anything within us that inspires duress. Going into relationship with our fears is a false means of maintaining "control" in our attempt to protect ourselves. The devil we know is better than the devil we don't. Acknowledging our feelings places us in a position of greater vulnerability, yet in our sensitivity, we are more accurate in assessing not only what is occurring within us, but around us -- therefore becoming more clear in defining our next course of action.

It's an irony of Spiritual Physics that by dismantling our own walls only then are we made impervious.

DAY 137
GREATEST ASSET

Change is our greatest asset though it often frightens us the most. When we relax into going with the flow of the current, we are less caught up with the peripheral activity occurring on the riverbank and much more focused on the direction of our own journey.

The current of change inspires invaluable life path focus.

DAY 138
MIRACLES ARE YOUR BIRTHRIGHT

There are times when our best ability to plan falls short as we simply don't have all the information needed. It is in those times of uncertainty when we are blinded by a lack of information; our are feet bound by the lack of path beneath them; our hands bound by a lack of purpose for them; our identity is crushed beneath a lack of relevance; it is during those times of darkness, restriction and stalemate when miracles are given their chance to work magic in our lives. Magic is real and happens when we let go. Not *give up* -- but let go. Never give up on Creation / God / Universe. Creation never gives up on us. Always make room for Miracles.

They are your birthright.

DAY 139
PAY ATTENTION

We can observe a great deal about a person in watching how they choose to handle another's pain --

-- when they themselves are feeling none.

DAY 140
KNOW THE DIFFERENCE

There is a difference between putting ourselves on the line for those we care about and attempting to "save" people who will not choose to save themselves. There is a difference between cutting a friend some slack while they are having a bad day and being used as a doormat. Discerning *why* we are being treated the way that we are being treated by another, rather than reacting over how we are *not* being treated, is key to understanding not only others, but ourselves. Emotionally over-correcting is just as self-destructive as emotionally under-correcting when it comes to making changes in our lives.

We are half of the puzzle in any relationship equation.

DAY 141
THE REASONS

There are, most definitely, reasons for everything. The Universe works in a manner more finely tuned than we are able to comprehend, each action netting a reaction, each ripple crossing over another ripple to create a third ripple of probability on an infinite level. Reading the "future" is a complex decoding process of this intricate space / time net, all of which is working in sync for the highest good of the entire system -- a system which is the sum total of all its parts. That all being said -- sometimes we just need to buck up, put our heads down, go straight into the storm, and hope for the best. As a species, we tend to over think most everything that causes us discomfort. Though we seek clarity on The Meaning Of It All, Cause and Effect, and Life Purpose -- this walk in life is all about how we handle the journey -- not why we purchased the tour. So cowboy up, Humanity. You've already bought the 100 year tour of Earth -- you may as well enjoy the twists and turns the tour offers. When we all signed on for this carnival ride, remember -- it did say in the fine print: *The Universe is not responsible for lost or stolen items, such as but not limited to dreams, courage, sense of self, direction, motivation, creativity --*

-- or sense of humor.

DAY 142
CENTER YOURSELF

Center yourself in all things that are good. Not because you can't withstand the bad or because you fear the bad but because as a Creation of Light -- the good is your Primary Operating System. It is home. It's easy to confuse "good" with "happy". Being centered in good doesn't always mean you'll be happy. But it does mean that you will be true to WHAT you are.

And WHAT you are in this incarnation is WHO you are.

DAY 143
PARTICIPATE

None of us are one-trick ponies. The moment we convince ourselves that we have only *one* purpose in this lifetime is the moment we teach ourselves to breathe through only one nostril at a time. It's simply not possible due to our design. We make choices our entire life. As such, we think we choose our path -- yet we don't. It often chooses us in spite of our choices.

It's simply our job to participate.

DAY 144
FOLLOW LOVE

Lead not with misunderstanding, for it breeds only confusion. Lead not with malice, for malice knows nothing else. Lead not with fear, for fear will lead you.

Instead follow love, which needs not ever lead.

DAY 145
WATCH THE TREAD

We must remember that in this human body, we are the *form* that *functions*, not the whole function. In other words, the wheel is not the miles that it travels, nor are the miles a reflection of the wheel. The wheel shows wear on the tread, and thus takes ownership of the miles. But the fact remains that the wear is only a reflection of two things: 1) the path's severity along the wheel's journey, and 2) the composition of the wheel. Life teaches us what we're made of by showing us areas in which we "wear", thus allowing us to learn how to approach any upcoming challenging terrain differently --

-- as not to leave too much of us behind on the road.

DAY 146
EGO VS SPIRIT

Our ego tells us that we are everything we've built.

Our spirit tells us to build with everything we are.

DAY 147
WHAT IS REAL?

All we have that can be considered *real* -- is happening right now. Literally. Reading this, your experience is REAL -- in this moment. Our memories, good and bad, are echoes within the canyons of our past. Worrying about the future is Theater in the Mind, a projection. Both the latter exist only in the matrix of our thoughts. The "right now", every single day we are given -- is REAL. So today, don't take action because of what you fear the future will hold or what you recall from the past. Take action TODAY on what TODAY requires. It will automatically shape your future and your life will be moved forward according to what it is meant to be --

--really.

DAY 148
TINY ADJUSTMENTS

The Universe is in the business of providing us with what we feel we deserve. Though bad things happen to good people, as long as we participate with a situation that does not suit our greatest good, we will continue to be disheartened with the results. If you would like to see change in your life, change how you handle your life. The Universe will honor even the most tiny of our adjustments to net us enormous results.

Don't be afraid to start small.

DAY 149
NOT YOUR PIG, NOT YOUR FARM

Usually, when we are doubted the most by others, it is an indication that others are the most doubting of themselves. Our emotional projection of "what's wrong with" someone else often times points right back at what's "wrong" with us. We must be wary of the fingers we point, as they almost always should be pointed toward an issue within. Those who cross a line in finding fault with others are seeking the fault line within themselves. We are not a blank canvass to receive the projection of fears and personal failures of another. We are beautiful, unique individuals, worthy of the dignity of being addressed for who we are -- not how we fit into another person's "most convenient idea" of who we are. The latter has nothing to do with us. We are not responsible to wear the caricatures of ourselves designed by others for their comfort level. Our only obligation is to our own authenticity.

Without accepting our own authenticity, there is no "life" or "relationship" that we may call our own.

DAY 150
DO, BE, HAVE

Do what is right -- and right outcome will follow. Be what is true -- and truth shall be brought to you. Have courage in the face of adversity --

-- and adversity will refuse to face you.

DAY 151
INSECURITY

Insecurity has a back door entrance directly into our soul. If we neglect to be diligent in checking the locks, it will open the door. If we neglect to be diligent in acknowledging the squeaking hinges, it will let itself in. If we neglect to be diligent in remembering our Design, it will become us.

Insecurity is an infestation, eradicated only by embracing fully who we are.

DAY 152
TO THE WORK

Be who you wish you were. If you can wish it, if you can envision it -- then you are capable of enacting it. You've already done so in your mind. Though our past can contain both amazing and painful memories, we are not restricted to only "what has been". We restrict ourselves because it is safer to ruminate on the past than venture onto the future. The best version of YOU is yet to come, even if the vision of such a path is not readily available. Time creates a give and take throughout our life. But in terms of the human spirit, time does nothing but appreciate our human value. If you are alive -- still walking this planet -- you aren't done yet. Universe still has a plan that you're part of, and you're still participating. You don't need to know all the answers. That's the job of Creation. You just be YOU -- because YOU are amazing. You can't do the work that Creator can do, and Creation won't do the work you're supposed to do. Ladies and gentlemen, welcome to the Free Will Ride here in the Third Dimension Theme Park. The ride leaves every moment you're alive, and the line starts right where you're at.

So you'll always be first.

DAY 153
POLARIZATION

People say that "without the dark, we would not know light". It's more accurate to say that without the Light, we would not see clearly through the Dark. Light cuts through the dark and removes it. That is its function. Human kind craves comparison in order to assign understanding. Light or dark, black or white, good or bad, happy or sad, the human spirit is the mixing pot of all things -- the Great Grey Area. Rest in your Grey.

Within your Grey lies the most accurate ability to discern any situation.

DAY 154
PAY IT FORWARD

Food for thought: "Pay-it-forward" can also apply to bad attitudes as well as good deeds. When someone else's garbage is dumped on your head, remember to take a breath before turning right around and dumping the garbage on someone else's head. Dumping on another is not acceptable simply because we're feeling lousy in our own skin at that moment. If we take responsibility for our own moods, then we won't feel the need to relegate other human beings as our own garbage disposals. We have no idea what another person has gone through that day prior to our need to dump on them. If the human race stopped paying forward bad attitudes just because it "felt good in the moment", we'd have evolved a lot further as a species. Hurt people -- *hurt* people. Make sure what you're paying forward today is a stepping stone, not a stumbling block. You'll feel better --

-- and so bettered will be your corner of the universe and all who are in it.

DAY 155
PERFECT DISTRACTION

Fear is the perfect distraction.

It keeps us occupied in a cage of our choosing while Life runs free ahead of us.

DAY 156
YOUR BEST

Do your best each day. And *best* is defined as giving all you have to give, *that day*. We are biological creatures, and every day we navigate different emotions, events, hormones, brain chemistry -- we are a walking, talking sack of reactive soup. Rather than reveling in the disappointment of not operating at peak capacity at all times, which is an unrealistic expectation, we must learn to accept each day as having a different "best" based on how we feel and what's occurring around us. It is in our greatest interest to view ourselves, and others, with this grace. If we are able to accept this *best* as truth, then we are also able to accept the fact that "perfect", like "best" -- has a fluid definition. Light views us as perfect, in all our imperfection. Darkness attempts to convince us that our imperfection disqualifies us from any form of *best*. We are at our best when we simple chose to BE.

It is not a competition from day to day.

DAY 157
REUNITING

Keep moving forward. If you can't remember what makes you happy, do something for someone else that you know will make *them* happy. We are reunited with our passion through reuniting others with their passion.

Remember -- Like attracts Like in Spiritual Physics.

DAY 158
LETTING GO

"Letting go" isn't about what you're leaving behind.

It's about making room for what's to come.

DAY 159
MEDITATION

Meditation for Today: Mother / Father Creator -- Bring blessing to our earth and every person on it, whether we agree with them or not. We are more the same than we are different, and we need one another to bring your ultimate vision for this planet *to* this planet. We are all an aspect of you. Bring blessing to the hurting heart of every individual, and bring peace to those who are tormented. Bring purpose to those who are lost. Clear the illusion from the eyes of those who struggle. Strengthen our Mother Earth and bolster the spirits and resolution of we who dwell upon her. And may you grant us the ability to love in the face of fear, to forgive one another, and moreover --

-- to forgive ourselves.

DAY 160
LISTEN

Listen to the tiny whisper inside of you. It is the voice of Creation, constantly beckoning you to your highest path, highest calling, your highest form of peace. We drown out this little voice out with personal agendas or the business of the day. Yet what we fear is change, not honoring our call.

Defining *why* we fear is the first step in clarifying our Purpose.

DAY 161
TRUE BRAVERY

True inner strength comes from acknowledging our own weaknesses. True inner courage comes from acknowledging our own fears. True humility comes from acknowledging the illusion of our own ego.

True bravery comes from choosing to live on the other side of acknowledgement.

DAY 162
DIFFERENT PLANETS

Each one of us is our own planet, complete with multiple cultures, languages, customs, biological systems, storms, plate shifts, and disasters. We cycle as a planet would: We experience tides (often subject to the moon), we have freak storm outbreaks that ruin everything, we poison our own water (with any number of sugars and alcohols), we pollute our air (cigarettes, cigars), and we fight with ourselves. Next time someone asks you if you think the human race could deal with meeting a being from another planet, answer "yes" because we do it every day --

-- every time we say hello to a stranger.

DAY 163
THE PHYSICS OF DISCERNMENT

Discernment is the better part of action. The key to discernment is removing our personal hopes, desires, and agenda as applied to the outcome of any situation, prior to forming a plan of action. The lack of doing so projects onto the situation our desired outcome as we re-write the situation according to our personal wishes, which may or may not have to do with the facts at hand. Discernment is a discipline.

Acting upon the discerned information is a choice.

DAY 164
FEARING THE WORLD

Don't be troubled by events that are not yours to control. There is a reason the machine has grown so big that it no longer can support its own weight: We only learn by doing. There are bigger pieces at play on the board and these are not ours to individually move. Instead, move the pieces right in front of you, without regard to how it affects the giant game going on overhead. The Game of the Machine is unaware of the millions of games below. Your winnings are yours alone and have nothing to do with the rest of the seizing system. See yourself as separate from the ship that is sinking --

-- and you will suddenly realize that you have never been attached to the deck.

DAY 165
TINY PEBBLES

You don't have to be the smartest, or most well-spoken, or best looking, or most influential, or the most wealthy person on the earth -- in order to change the world. The tiniest pebble in the shoe of a giant will change the journey --

-- altering the path one step at a time.

DAY 166
LOVE TRANSFORMS

Love is the most transformational force in this third dimension. You have an unlimited supply so leave love everywhere you go -- especially with the people closest to you. We are taught to expend the best of ourselves on professional alliances, political relationships, and strangers, so those closest to us receive the "daily scraps". The moment we take for granted those who are part of our foundation --

-- the rest of our empire crumbles under folly.

DAY 167
CONFRONT DIFFICULTIES

We can pack away our issues with others on ice to deal with later, but don't forget about them. Otherwise, months later, we'll stumble upon them, all shoved to the back of our emotional refrigerator, and what was once a neat package that could be sorted and thrown away is now a rotted mess that's spoiled the whole shelf. The clean up is then ten times harder. Confronting difficulties with others is hard. But living day to day in the rot of the situation is harder --

-- as well as an emotional health hazard.

DAY 168
YOUR MIGRATION

It's okay if you wake up and decide that the course of your life should be changed. It doesn't mean you've "wasted" time up to this point; it means that you are now ready to make the change because you've now notice the need. This is a migratory time for the human race as our expansion is not "Westward" --

-- but "Inward".

DAY 169
KNOW THYSELF

The truth is as powerful a healer as love. It's often hard to come by, mostly because we fear the weight of what truth represents: Accountability. We sell white lies to ourselves more than anyone else in our life yet demand "truth" from our loved ones, our business associates, and our family. This inconsistency in expectation vs. personal action nets tough karmic lessons of Illusion and Deception in our daily life. Today, try telling the truth to yourself and come out of judgment with your answer. How do you REALLY feel about how YOU conduct yourself and your life? If you find you're being negative just to be "humble", or you find you're being positive because the affirmations say so -- stop. Now. Ask yourself again: How do you really feel about how you conduct yourself and your life? Are you mostly in authenticity? Mostly in fear? Are you mostly in The Self, or mostly in others? The only "wrong" answer is the untruthful one. Know thyself. Accept what you can't change, love what you've worked hard towards, and improve areas that make you uncomfortable within yourself.

We cannot expect committed authenticity from others when we ourselves are unwilling to commit to our own.

DAY 170
PURPOSE OF A BREAKING HEART

It is only when the heart is broken wide open --

-- that the Light is able to reach all the crevices within.

DAY 171
PATH OF PURPOSE

Success and stature are positive side-effects of a job well done, yet we must never lose sight of our Primary Design. Our desires originate from our heart, yet if we become our desires and leave behind our heart, the foundations of our very endeavors are built upon the sands of illusion. We are *who we are* FIRST and *what we are* SECOND. Who we are is what we are. If what we are betrays who we are, then we've strayed off the Path of Purpose and into the Arena of Ego.

The moment we claim our identity as *what* we are, we put the Universe's best plans for us on hold, as we are not *who* we are, to receive them.

DAY 172
LIVE THE CHANGE

When we choose to let go of the pain that we have carried, many experience a "hole" in their lives. Suffering is the companion with whom many spend 24 hours a day, 7 days a week. To fill the "hole", people will sometimes revert back to a hurtful situation simply to experience that familiar "relationship". If you are making positive changes by weeding out the hurt in your life, make sure to dive into new activities and fantastic friends to fill out your daily rotation.

To make a change, we must live the change.

DAY 173
FAITH ON CREDIT

Faith is the act of extending credit to anything or anyone --

-- without first requiring an application.

DAY 174
FAITH ON CREDIT

Just when you're certain that Life is trying to break your back, stone by stone, day by day, you'll find the impending "pile of rock" is actually the foundation of a vaulting palace. Our greatest rewards are the direct result of our greatest duress. Even more often, we are unable to see the shape of these rewards until we accept that the exercise is not about enduring the weight of each stone, but in accepting the strength of our resolve. If you feel that life has you "buried" beneath its weight -- hang in there.

You're about to be made aware of all that has been built for you in the meantime.

DAY 175
QUALITY CONTROL

We are not going to be every single person's "cup of tea", no matter how hard we try. So relax. Not everyone will like you. Not everyone will understand you. Not everyone will want to be your friend. And that's okay. That leaves more room in your life for the people who will love you for *exactly* who you are.

Think of it as Universal Quality Control.

DAY 176
HOPEFUL

Don't be afraid to feel positive and hopeful -- especially right now! Give it all you've got! To be hopeful is not to be in denial about facing difficulties.

It is the momentum needed to run all the way up the hill.

DAY 177
TRUE NORTH

When you feel a nagging pull in one direction, even if that direction makes no sense at the time, there is generally a profound reason. While Life tends to shout illusion in our face, Spirit whispers truth to our soul. The compass needle neither decides nor strategizes its direction, but instead is pulled by mere design to align with True North. If Spirit has set in motion a system where even the compass is automatically set to right course, surely we, with our resounding treasure trove of invaluable gifts, talents, and incredible relevance to the world, are designed to automatically align with our True North. When your internal compass needle swings, know it is the pull of Spirit righting your course.

Take courage in embarking upon your new and undiscovered journey.

DAY 178
FORGED STRONG

We cannot save others from themselves. Nor can they save us from ourselves. None of us wish to see the other in pain. Yet our job is not to rob one another of our lessons. Hard knocks come harder when our "help" becomes a hinder. We must be allowed to plummet down our own learning curve and experience the inertia No one would wait in line for the roller coaster ride if not for the fear of the first crest.

In this inertia, like a sword forged by relentless yet purposeful pounding, are we sharpened and tempered to unyielding strength.

DAY 179
JEALOUSY

The Universe is a perfect provider. We all have to remember that what is ours is ours. It is meant for us. What is meant for another is theirs and meant for them. Jealousy is based on the fear of being invisible --

-- a wasted emotion whose only purpose is to create the illusion that we are each trapped inside of a cage, without supplies.

DAY 180
MIND AND PURPOSE

A clear mind and a clear purpose --

-- are the only true looking glass for the soul.

DAY 181
SYSTEM OF LIGHT

Don't worry about *what* could be coming. Worry instead for those who don't see *you* coming. You are more capable and more powerful than you even know how to quantify. Your Light is your key code through any door. Where your code is not valid, your Light is protected. Have faith.

The System of Light has been in place long before we ever were.

DAY 182
GROW YOURSELF

Spread your wings, shine brightly to your fullest capacity, and be exactly who you are. This will threaten some, and inspire others. Be accountable for your shortcomings and do not lay blame. This will be viewed as weakness by some, and earn respect from others. Extend a helping hand then move along if your help is not desired. This will be seen as betrayal by some, and strength by others. Forgive yourself so that you may do the same for those around you. This will anger some, and heal others. Hold compassion for everyone, for you don't know the cost of their journey. This will be resented by some, and embraced by others. Above all, never be afraid to love with everything you have. Some simply cannot accept it, and others will be ignited.

You cannot grow anyone but yourself.

DAY 183
OURSELVES, DEFINED

Who we are in this life does not define our Purpose.

It is our Purpose in this life that defines who we are.

DAY 184
LOVE FEARLESSLY

Give in to your need to love. It's your greatest attribute, the ability to love someone so much that your heart bursts. It takes strength to admit that love makes us weak in the knees. It takes strength to make room for another.

Love fearlessly.

DAY 185
GOSSIP AND HEARSAY

Gossip, hearsay, and the "tabloid mentality" that fuels "group think" is one of the most influential tools of The Dark. When we make personal and professional decisions based upon gossip, hearsay, and mob modalities, we make a decision to abandon our own spiritual calling toward a higher purpose. We abandon our conscience and take on a life path governed the fear of a lack of acceptance. Do not seek gossip as entertainment. Do not accept hearsay as truth. Do not adopt the mob mentality for fear of being ostracized by the group think. Have courage to back away, even quietly, from situations where ugliness is not only supported but encouraged.

To turn a blind eye to the injustices exacted toward to any one of us then grants The Universe permission to lay upon us the very same.

DAY 186
SURRENDER

We are all free, even encouraged, to chart and navigate our own course across the Waters of Life.

Yet the most efficient route always involves surrendering to the current.

DAY 187
THE TRICK TO LIFE

The trick to life is that there isn't one. And that's perfectly okay. You don't need tricks to get through the day. All you need to know is that there are plenty of people in your life who believe that you matter -- even if you don't believe this to be true. Our biggest fan is Creation Itself.

There's no "trick" to the fact that you've earned all this love.

DAY 188
EMOTIONAL HEALING

Emotional healing is a complicated process. It demands that we review our past. However, we should never be so fixated on the missteps in our past that the present is lost in a never-ending sea of resentment, mistrust, or martyrdom. That is not "healing", but reliving the very same past that has brought us to the current state of pain. Healing involves letting go. Not condoning, but letting go. Letting go involves forgiveness. Not forgetfulness, but forgiveness.

Until we can truly forgive ourselves, and then others, healing will never be ours.

DAY 189
ASK YOURSELF

Where there is inner peace, there is beauty in the world. Where there is beauty in the world, there is peace. The very nature of The System is designed to propagate the perpetual motion of wellness, and this wellness starts within the soul of each one of us. In fact, the Spiritual System is so stacked toward resolution and peace that we must work very hard to continue to bring unrest into our reality. Consider how many hours in the day are spent on unrest. Consider the daily energy exerted in worry, discontent and anger. Now consider the hours that could be used in Peace. And consider that it is not mandatory for humanity to learn through pain, though we often choose that lesson. The fact that humanity often cannot envision a life without painful struggle is perhaps the most mind-boggling thought of all. So ask yourself:

If you could request of the Universe lessons that did NOT include a painful learning curve, would you consider those lessons as "valid" as the lessons which involved pain?

DAY 190
STAY FREE

Without challenges, we never truly understand our capacity to overcome. There is great freedom in enacting our strengths.

Be Strong. Stay Free.

DAY 191
EMBRACE YOU

Today, take pride in every single thing you've ever done in your life, good or bad -- to bring you to this point. Without having the courage to face your life day to day, you would not be the magnificent, complicated, and beautiful creature you are today. You are just right in all of your steps and missteps. If we were designed to be perfect, we wouldn't be Human at all. Embrace YOU.

The Universe does.

DAY 192
PERSONAL REJECTION

Letting go is hard. Though there is a time to fight for what we believe in or what we have built, there is also discernment in accepting that our participation is no longer desired. Doors close for a reason. We are often told directly to our face, and even shown in the lack of enthusiasm present in others with regard to our contribution with jobs, teams, and even personal relationships, that our time or contribution to the situation is no longer required. Yet we refuse to accept the transition because we mistake the Universal Nod of Completion as "personal rejection". Therefore, in seeking relevance to the situation that once defined us, we continue to bang our hearts, gifts, and most stunning and valuable attributes against a pathway, relationship, or job that is no longer open to us. This inequity in perception is often very painful. If we are not needed or desired in any given situation and we have given the situation our "everything" -- then accepting this fact without the danger of emotionally judging ourselves is important. We cannot force others to agree that our value is relevant to their path, nor should we.

The lesson then becomes not about surviving closed doors but about our most invigorating re-direction.

DAY 193
TRY

In terms of Spiritual Physics, doing the *very best* you can is as good as a *win*.

The only time you lose is when you don't try at all.

DAY 194
LEAN FORWARD

Many times, "doing the right thing" is far more frightening than doing nothing. The act of standing in the gap for those without a voice is a courageous exercise of the spirit but often feels unsupported in the moment, much like falling face-first off of a cliff. In order to overcome this fear, so that you may "do the right thing", relax into the plummet. Lean forward with your right actions and allow the gravity of the situation to do the rest.

You are not responsible for gravity.

DAY 195
WATCH INTENTION

The old saying "actions speak louder than words" is half accurate. The other half is "energy speaks louder than words". Always pay close attention to the energy behind any action. Within the energy lies motive, and within motive lies intention.

Within intention lies the answer to everything.

DAY 196
INTO THE LIGHT

Stepping onto the Path of Light is sometimes an unpopular social decision. When we remain tucked away in the shadows, it is much easier to assume we fit into any form that others wish to project onto us -- as we look like almost anything in the Dark. When we step into the Light, every detail of our being is illuminated. To those who are also in the Light, this is welcome, as they can now clearly see us for who we are. For those in the shadows, we suddenly appear to be completely different as all of our details are revealed. The truth is that we are no different. We are simply being seen for exactly who we are, rather than for the identity that Darkness has projected onto us for its convenience. The action of our stepping into the Light is often polarizing for those who remain in shadows as it challenges them to accept the fine details within themselves -- details that by staying in the shadows, they may be avoiding. By stepping onto a path of Light, we courageously own every ounce of our being.

In this courage, we inspire self-acceptance, self-love, and illumination in others.

DAY 197
RE-START THE PENDULUM

We are so accustomed to "pendulum thinking" -- expecting everything to swing back once it has swung too far to one side -- that we tend to wait for results rather than take action to achieve results. There is a time for pause and a time for effort. Sometimes the pendulum can't "swing back" because its platform has been tilted due to how wide it has rocked. Like righting an off-balance clock, we must discern when it's time to level the platform.

Re-starting the pendulum sometimes requires adjusting the foundation.

DAY 198
YOU ARE WORTH IT

Incase no one has told you lately: YOU are WORTH IT. It's not just in your head -- you really ARE gifted and very special in your own way, solely unique unto you. You are supposed to be here, even if it doesn't feel like it lately. The Universe believes in you. Creator loves you more than you can imagine. Even when you feel invisible -- you are never invisible to that which made you, and those who truly know your heart.

Now go do something glorious, rock star. It's your world, after all!

DAY 199
ANGEL UP FRONT

Don't let the devil you create in your mind--

-- shout louder than the angel standing right in front of you.

DAY 200
FEAR OF CHANGE

Clinging to what we used to be in times of great transition is much like hugging the railing of a sinking ship. Once the ship has lost its ability to keep us afloat, it's time to let go. So it is with our evolution as individuals. People either fall away from the "fear of change" in order to embrace their highest design, or people lose their minds within the fear of change while clinging to their own folly. Allow yourself to grow in a positive way while experiencing change. This change in YOU may seem uncertain, or even "scary", simply because it doesn't resemble the last version of yourself that you're more familiar with. We are designed to grow and change throughout our lifetime in order to stay afloat. Otherwise, we become nothing more than an effigy to ourselves, a walking caricature of our past --

-- set adrift on a sinking vessel whose hull has been damaged in our many wars with ourselves.

DAY 201
LOVE

Love:

Choose it or Lose it.

DAY 202
GRATITUDE FOR HELP

Make sure to be grateful today for all those who have ever helped you on your journey, no matter how big the contribution. You may not be where you want to be in life right now, but your path -- your "success" -- is a cumulative work in progress. Our success is not solely ours, but the result of Team Universe's effort -- of which, we are only part. So do your part. Yet always enact gratitude when acknowledging that many others have done their part on your behalf, in one way or another. If you've progressed forward in life at all -- you've had help. Even if you feel isolated, you're not an island. The proof?

An Island never moves.

DAY 203
UNIVERSAL NEED

We all want to be loved for exactly who we are, and forgiven for what we are not.

Therein lies the one Universal need that defines the human spirit.

DAY 204
SCHOOL OF LIFE

Mistakes, wrong turns, missteps, hurtful words and selfish actions are all tough payments toward our tuition in the School of Life. By learning what doesn't work, we learn what does.

If we embrace our education during this Human Experience, we graduate this lifetime with a Bachelors Degree in Love, a Masters in Compassion, and a Doctorate in Self-Forgiveness.

DAY 205
USE YOUR POWER

Be good and do good. Allow all others in between the room to learn at their own pace. We can't save others from themselves. A fool with a rope will inevitably find a tall tree. Do we then burn all rope, or cut down all forests, simply because one may hang themselves? It is not within our power to take away someone else's life lessons. It is, however, within our power to be part of another's lesson. In this participation lies our power to make a difference.

Use your power wisely.

DAY 206
PERSPECTIVE

Allow yourself the room to grow past what scares you.

It's amazing how the mountain looks like a speed bump in the rear view mirror.

DAY 207
NEEDS

There are certain things in life that we think we "need" in order to validate our careers, our lives, or our relationships. However, the moment we let go of these preconceived "needs", we've validated our careers, our lives and our relationships by acknowledging their worth in the present. To wait on "needs" being fulfilled in order to claim happiness is to continually seek validation from the future. This validation will never arrive if we cannot validate today --

-- as only today builds our tomorrow.

DAY 208
RE-PLANTING

Allow yourself the room to grow then allow The Universe to re-plant you where you belong.

Faith means having the courage to let your roots dangle as you're pulled from the seedling pot and placed into more fertile ground.

DAY 209
TENSION

When we encounter a challenge the likes of which we've never seen, The Universe is not inflicting suffering, but instead, pointing us to our strengths. A suspension bridge, such as The Golden Gate in San Francisco, maintains its strength from the stress placed upon thousands of tiny wire strands within the main cables. It is the balance of tension and weight that connects two sides. Sometimes, while crossing a bridge in our lives, tension *is* the strength --

-- but only while bearing the weight of the journey from point A to point B.

DAY 210
FORGIVE

The most important thing you'll ever do is forgive yourself for wishing that you were "more". The most compassionate thing you'll ever do is forgive those who taught you this behavior.

The most loving thing you'll ever do is forgive those who have no idea how to do either.

DAY 211
JUST DO

Any success in your future starts with one action today. Even the great pyramids were constructed one block at a time. Simply DO one action toward your goal everyday, rather than THINK of twenty. Don't stand at the base of the mountain and, in your mind, pre-count the steps it takes to reach the top.

You'll wear yourself out on the idea of the climb and never make the journey.

DAY 212
REACHING OUT

We often reach out to others hoping that what we receive back will in some way validate the effort of our attempt to reach out. Yet to truly "reach out" means to not expect anything in return. The human condition often struggles with third party validation. We all require validation, yet sometimes, we seek it from sources that simply cannot provide what we are seeking.

Today, if you "reach out" to another, look at it as a one-way ticket, and be joyful for the ride there.

DAY 213
WORDS HAVE WEIGHT

It's not just a myth or an allegory -- words have actual spiritual weight. They frame up the energy of a thought in a time capsule so that it may be transferred. That thought can then either become a weighted bullet or a warm blanket -- both options have a physical affect on the person delivering the words and the person receiving them. Never misspeak so viciously that the weight of the words outweighs the apology.

A scale so tipped is incredibly difficult to right.

DAY 214
LOOK UP

Look to the skies for inspiration, for if the random wind can sculpt figures from clouds --

-- the purposeful hand of The Universe can surely shape the most chaotic of situations into a glorious and defining moment.

DAY 215
DISEASES

Hatred is a disease of the mind. Greed is a disease of the body. Apathy is a disease of the spirit. When Mind-Body-Spirit is in DIS-ease, one can CHOOSE ease by applying cures that are created by the heart: Forgiveness for Hatred, Acceptance for Greed, and Empathy for Apathy.

Forgiveness, Acceptance, and Empathy: the Triple Threat against Darkness.

DAY 216
EXCITEMENT

Where there are needs of the many, there is work excited to be done. Where there is pain to the many, there is compassion excited to be delivered. Where there is hope that has been lost, there is encouragement excitedly waiting in the wings. Like a rising tide, Light overtakes everything in its wake -

-- and you are unsinkable in It's waters.

DAY 217
OBSERVE YOUR ACTIONS

You're not a "waste of time" for someone else. Your ability to feel is not "too much". You're not the sum total of your resume, or the letters behind your name. Instead, you are exactly *who* you are. The key to understanding *who* is in the understanding of *what* you are. And to understand *what*, observe your everyday actions. We are defined by how we choose to behave in this life, everyday. What we are is how we act.

And how we act defines our world.

DAY 218
WORK AT IT

Anyone can be made into a Rock Star. Being "made" means nothing. The true Lathe of Character lies in mastering the grunt work in one's own life. True Stardom is achieved when one no longer cares if it ever is. True Success is achieved whenever you're ready to accept that you are the only one authoring that success.

Now get to work.

DAY 219
EMPATHY

Expecting others to understand our joys, our pain, our fears, our ups, our downs, our journey -- is much like expecting a three-year-old to understand proper dinner table etiquette: We will always end up disappointed. No matter how observant or how intuitive we are, we will never have the capability to know another person's life. The very best we can offer one another is EMPATHY for what each of us is experiencing. Throwing solutions or platitudes at a person who is hurting is often not about "assisting" that person but about making ourselves feel better in the moment -- rather than sitting in the pain with the individual who is experiencing suffering. "If there's anything I can do" communicates just the opposite. It informs the person who is hurting that that we are not willing to do something THEN, in their deepest moment of need, to help them. It indicates that they must wait for our emotional participation. It is a bookmark that allows us feel better as we sidestep emotional involvement. Just as waiting to put out a fire will allow a fire to grow, this action serves no purpose. "Fixing" is an emotional distancing tool we use that enables us to feel as if we've "done something". It is our own conscience cleanser. It is about us -- what WE can do in that moment -- not the person in pain. It is the emotional equivalent of "throwing money" at a child instead of simply sharing yourself with them. Empathizing is about taking time with someone, truly listening, and having the courage to share the emotional burden, if only for a moment.

Empathy is having the strength to connect, listen, and share.

DAY 220
REMINDERS

Allow the Spirit of Peace to flow through your veins like warm hope. Invite harmony with kind action. Inspire trust in others by trusting yourself. Love without rules or restrictions. Give because it feels good in your tummy. Sing even if you think you can't, just because it's fun. Laugh at yourself because we are all perfect in our imperfections. Hug mercilessly. Compliment those who cannot muster a compliment. Listen through the pain in a friend's voice. Comfort even when you don't understand the ache.

Connect. Create. Grow. Live.

DAY 221
PEACE

Peace is not simply a state of being, nor a state of mind. Peace is not simply an action. Peace, in its truest native form, is a Spirit -- one that overtakes the being, the mind, and all actions. May the Spirit of Peace fill you as water overflows a chalice.

And may a garden of love grow at your feet.

DAY 222
RECOMMENDED DAILY USE

Love is an all-purpose tool. An unfathomably effective adhesive, blanket, attractant, repellent, bridge, food, fuel, billboard, bullhorn, salve, life vest, ladder, shield or shelter, always apply love liberally. In case of accidental contact with nose or eyes, spontaneous tears of joy may occur followed by snorting laughter.

Okay to use while operating heavy machinery, especially the human body.

DAY 223
SURVIVAL

Between the weight and agony of our pain lies the Silence that whispers to us --

-- the love that keep us breathing.

DAY 224
RECEIVE HELP

By opening yourself spiritually and mentally to the possibility that your most streamlined plan for your life may not even represent one tiny portion of your total capabilities (some of which you may not even be aware of without being challenged to bring them forward), you then open yourself to the notion that perhaps -- just perhaps -- a Force greater than yourself has a Plan even more exquisite than your best strategy. This does not mean that we are lacking free will. It does not mean you're a "puppet" in some grand scheme beyond your control. It means that you are accepting of the HELP that is possible from a Source that has far more data on our lives, ourselves, and our surroundings than even we do. We will blindly follow a GPS navigational device even against our knowledge that the map is wrong -- yet we dig our heels into the sand when it comes to receiving Spiritual GPS assistance. The only difference in receiving the two is our Ego. The Ego does not take ownership of a City Map, yet we "own" the map of our life because we are creating the route as we go. Once we recognize that the map of our life (our North-South-East-West overview) is not always penned by us, but utilized by us to navigate, it's much easier to accept Spiritual Assistance through our own inner GPS. If you find yourself going into opposition with using your own "Spiritual Onstar" once you are turned around in the maze of your own infinite choices, ask yourself: If I were lost in an unfamiliar city -- would I seek help finding my way back to the interstate?

Or would I waste my gas driving to and fro?

DAY 225
YOU ARE THE STAR

Remain true to who and what you are. Your Universe is shifting around you to place the right staircase at your feet so that you may ascend above the moon you once saw as distant. You are the star you've been wishing upon. You are the dream you have strived to achieve. Heaven is within you.

It always has been.

DAY 226
WORRY

There is no point in the energy of "worry". Worrying is the action of creating fictitious scenarios within the mind and accepting an emotional response from them as if they were real. Worry is chewing gum for the psyche -- something we do that nets us no nutritional value yet uses energy. Worrying is an exercise in the acceptance of illusion as reality -- which, in part, is the definition of a delusion. When we CHOOSE to participate in worry, we are choosing to participate in a delusion of the spirit and the mind. When we choose a fear-based reality and allow our bodies to experience anxiety -- as if the fictional storyline known as "worry" were really happening -- we create our own worst nightmare. Thus, we are the architects of our own Hell, authoring our own demons which torment us in our most tender places. Who better to terrify us in our most secret frightened places -- than ourselves? Let go of worry. It's not real. As such, it does not affect outcome. It is only a teaching tool if we require the lesson of self-delusion in order to learn trust. Instead, replace worried THOUGHTS with positive right ACTION.

The future writes itself as we allow our daily actions to build the platform on which our highest thoughts launch.

226

DAY 227
PURPOSE

The key to Your Purpose: Root yourself in your purpose and all life path issues will right themselves. Obstacle cannot stand against purpose. If you're not sure what your purpose is, root yourself in what gives you joy. Therein lies your purpose. If you're not sure what gives you joy, root yourself in bringing others joy. Through their joy you will find your own, and through your own joy you will find your purpose. Do your best not to dismiss your purpose because it's "not practical", "won't make you money", "don't have enough time" -- who says any of that is true, but you? Universe will always find a way to support your purpose as it is your cog in It's machine, and Universe is in the business of running smoothly. If anything, be prepared for your purpose, the thing that gives you the most joy -- to be something you never thought would. We often have an "idea" of our purpose based on what our low ego finds the most impressive or what we enjoy, unaware of what our greatest joy truly is. Be flexible in your joy, be flexible with your ego, and open to something new that you never even considered would bring you bliss.

The key to finding your purpose is accepting joy where you least expect it -- and running with it.

DAY 228
PRIORITIES

Just love. All else falls behind this. Be love. Enact love. Embrace love, give love. Where there is love, no unrest can flourish. Love is the thing that all others are measured against. Just love.

All else falls behind this.

DAY 229
PURPOSE

Within each one of us lies an ideal, what we each consider "the perfect life". Yet keep in mind that even this "perfect snapshot" is only that -- an image of what we THINK will make us the most happy. Ironically, it is not THINKING which fulfills the Human Spirit, but DOING. If you doubt this, consider that our spirit has chosen to live in a three-dimensional environment inhabiting a three-dimensional body which is capable of creating three-dimensional things. We are made to manifest three dimensionally, though we are capable of comprehending far more than three dimensions. Why this lesson in DOING? Because the Human Spirit is made in the Impression of Creation, and we excel when we CREATE. So today, if you're feeling stagnant, depressed, dead-ended, hopeless or powerless, remember: To kick that feeling, DO something in this third dimension. Clean a room. Wash your car. Bake something for someone else. Write a poem. Work out. Run an errand. Walk the dog. To escape the Prison of Limitation, we must leave the mind which created it and step outside the self --

-- into Application of the Self.

DAY 230
CHOOSE JOY

Be vigilant in your Joy. No one has the power to steal FROM you that which is created BY you. There is great power in your ability to CHOOSE Joy in the face of challenge. That doesn't mean ignoring pain or danger. It also doesn't mean being in denial about a difficult situation. Choosing Joy is an issue of Spiritual Physics. It means choosing strength through positive focus instead of allowing strength to be drained through negative association. We are created by Light, in the Image of Light, with an Operating System of Light. We're made to overcome through POSITIVE action. We're not designed to "be happy" all the time. Struggle appears to be part of the Human Learning Curve. However, we can choose joy as a means to deal with the weight of struggle. Try giving up the Illusion of Hopelessness and instead, inserting Joy for All That Is Working In Your Life -- even if it's something small.

Then watch the positive results roll in.

DAY 231
YOU ARE INFINITE

The best thing that you have to offer in life -- is YOU. You are enough for any task, any job, anyone. If you receive information contrary to that fact, it's nothing but static, white noise in the background of someone else's struggle. You are brilliant and capable, creative and interesting. You are a walking, talking miracle. Be the "infinite" you were created to be.

It's your zone.

DAY 232
DEPROGRAMMING

Rising to the occasion to allow our greatest strengths to become our "norm" is a learned behavior. We are often taught at a young age, by observing those around us, that our weaknesses will define us. For instance, we won't be happy because we'll be broke. We won't find love because it's scary to trust. We won't succeed because our dreams aren't real. These implied ideals become our reality until we deprogram ourselves from this Cult of Limitation in which we have been born. Your greatest strengths -- hope, love, and dreams -- are far more real than the energy it takes to debunk them. Trust the Spiritual Physics beneath the Fear.

It is the foundation on which all things are built.

DAY 233
HOW TO GIVE

Being yourself is the greatest gift you can give to anyone -- especially yourself. So embrace who you are. It's who Universe created you to be, for a reason. Embrace yourself so you can embrace others. Love yourself so you'll know how to love others. Have forgiveness for yourself so you'll know how to forgive others. Have fun with yourself so you'll know how to have fun with others. Compliment yourself so you'll know how to compliment others.

We must first learn how to accept in order to truly give.

DAY 234
DIRECTIONS

Ultimately, the path beneath your feet --

-- is the direction you've been looking for.

DAY 235
THE CIRCLE OF LOVE

With love comes trust. With trust comes risk. With risk comes fear. With fear comes anger. With anger comes forgiveness. With forgiveness comes motivation. With motivation comes strength. With strength comes courage. With courage comes action. With action comes inspiration. With inspiration comes creation. With creation comes inclusion. With inclusion comes connection. With connection -- comes love.

Love: A circle in action which cannot be broken.

DAY 236
SPIRITUAL GROWTH CHART

How to tell where you are at on the spiritual growth chart: If you blame another for emotions that surface within you -- you're in The Self. If you blame yourself for emotions that surface within you, you're in The Self. If you stop blaming anyone and simply accept that the emotions within you are your greatest teacher, you're in The Zone. Make friends with your fear and your pain. They are here to point you to areas within where you hide truths from yourself --

-- often about how to heal and move forward into your greatest purpose.

DAY 237
CHECKLIST

Be love. Be compassion. Be open. Be non-judgmental. Be honest. Be forgiveness. Be free of the illusion of control. Be patient. When you can't be patient -- be kind. You won't improve the lives of others by checking these items off of your list.

You'll improve yours.

DAY 238
ADDICTION TO ASSUMPTION

When we feel that someone hasn't communicated clearly, the responsibility is ours to speak up. We have such a habit of "assuming" that we'd rather jump to the worst conclusion rather than simply requesting clarification. The bigger issue, even greater than that of miscommunication, is our addiction to assumption. Human beings often feel the need to convince ourselves that others think the worst of us. In fact, it is we who think the worst of ourselves --

-- unwittingly casting another person in the role of the villain that will speak the script written by our own insecurities.

DAY 239
WILLINGNESS

Always give of yourself. It costs you nothing more than willingness. Without being willing, we are as brittle as window panes in winter --

-- shattering when too much warmth attempts to shine through.

DAY 240
PERSONAL DESIGN

What we are is who we are. To understand this concept fully, we must first be acquainted with what we are *not*. We are not the external world. We are not material possessions. We are not the choice of another individual to marry us. We are not the money in our bank account. We are not the cars in our driveway. We are not the title on our door. We are not the promotion for which we are striving. We are not the record deal. We are not the clothes and the jewelry we've accrued. We are not how many albums we sell or how many films in which we are cast. All of those items are mere reflections of our efforts, not our identity. Those efforts may or may not fall within our Purpose, yet our identity always falls within our Purpose. Our Personal Design is indelibly stamped within our spirit. Our Personal Design is not a matter of fate, but a skill set with which we are blessed, that when best set to purpose --

-- will net life-altering results not only for ourselves but for others around us.

DAY 241
REACH FOR LOVE

Reach for love. If it's not there in the drawer marked "romance", reach for the folder marked "family". If you can't find that file, open the box called "friends". If that box is empty, reach inside your heart. There is more love inside of YOU than you will ever realize. If you ever doubt that, remember: You can't long for something you've never had. You wouldn't know the difference in order to miss what you're longing for. Reach for love.

It's only as far away as your heart.

DAY 242
FAITH AND GRACE

Assumption is a deceptive playmate. It's a statement on the instant gratification of our digital age that when one doesn't receive a response right away, be it because they texted or emailed or left a message, they assume the person they left the message for is angry at them. And, it's a statement on the passive-aggressive nature of society that people interpret "silence" as "anger". Life is a busy thing and just because someone can't right get back to you, it doesn't mean they're angry. Try a more balanced approach: If you're not hearing from someone right away, it's likely because they're not in a position to respond, be it emotional, physical, or psychological. The more we separate our insecurities and egos from another person's process and realize someone's actions are not "all about us", the better off we all are.

Faith in others, with Grace, is the key.

DAY 243
FREEDOM

Revenge is a poison. It is not up to us to enact justice on another, but to act in a way that would inspire justice. Many times, when we are wounded in the heart by those who we consider careless, we feel we must wound back in order to heal. Striking out when we are hurting only creates a ripple of hurt, a wave in the timeline that will ultimately slap back against our own shoreline, splashing us with our own misdeeds. Hurt people will "hurt people:" Instead of reacting with malice and pain towards those who have reacted towards us out of their own malice and pain -- defuse the cycle of suffering with kindness. Offer to take a friend for a drive. Take yourself shopping. Purchase a beverage for a family member and bring it to them unexpectedly. Spiritual Physics dictate that for every intention there is a balancing intention -- much like Physics that state "for every action there is a reaction". If someone is putting malice through victimization into the Ethers, then balance that intention not with revenge, but with kindness. This action frees us from the role of "victim" and moves us out of the crosshairs of any negative energy. By balancing the energies in our own life, we release ourselves from the illusion of the shackles placed upon us by another.

We become free.

DAY 244
STAY CLEAR

Open your heart. Your entire Chakra system is designed much like a jet engine, sucking in energy from the back and propelling energy out the front. Nothing downs a 747 faster than catching a goose in an engine while trying to take off. Blocking our heart chakra in order to keep our most tender places protected then wreaks havoc on our energetic system which is designed to continue to circulate energy in order to keep us emotionally, spiritually, and intellectually healthy. Blocking our heart chakra is like attempting to plug a volcano: Nature will always prevail yet the consequences may level a few counties --

-- never mind what will be left of the tattered mountain after it blows.

DAY 245
MAKE ROOM

We cannot change another's opinion. Only another may choose that action. We spend countless hours, days, weeks, months, worrying about how to present our "case" to another so that they may see the world through the same perspective as we do. This is simply not possible. We are obsessed with others sharing our opinions because we feel justified in our own outlook when others agree with us. Instead of becoming angry with those who disagree with our outlook, consider that our anger is not with them, but in our own insecurity within as we worry that our personal outlook may indeed not be correct. We are not required to agree with every person we meet nor with every perspective that we run across. However, to be able to rest in our differences enables each of us to examine a different side of the same issue. In this examination from all angles lies the most clear picture of any given situation. To make room for another's opinion, even if we disagree, is not to negate our own.

It is to prove to the Self that we stand firmly in our own beliefs.

DAY 246
REMEMBER WHY

You are not invisible. You are not disposable. Your needs matter. Your heart is precious. Your dreams are valid. You are not wasting your time on this Earth. Remember why you chose to come here, to inhabit a physical body and have a physical experience: You knew you could make a difference. Even if that difference is within yourself. Celebrate your decision to experience a few bumps in the road in order to build a superhighway straight to your Highest Purpose. You are brilliant and capable. Accept this truth. Remember who you *are*.

All other illusion of who you are *not* will fall away.

DAY 247
REMAIN IN BALANCE

There is a time for focusing on the self and a time for focusing on the masses. We must remain in balance. When our journey with the self becomes obsession with the self, we become emotionally incestuous and all other relationships suffer. There is not one of us greater than the other in our pain, our struggle, our suffering, our joys, our accomplishments, our journeys, or our fears. None of us have earned a pass to crush those we have chosen to have in our life simply because we are hurting. That type of emotional entitlement is symptomatic of Darkness that has been left unattended in the Human Spirit. It's a choice to be a stumbling block rather than a stepping stone, not only in someone else's life, but in the realm of the Universal flow. The Universe seeks to eradicate resistance. If we choose to cause resistance --

-- that is a battle on whose losing end we will always land.

DAY 248
DAILY ACCOUNTABILITY LIST

How to avoid throwing others under the bus in a time of crisis:

1) Own your issues.
2) Listen while others air grievances.
3) Acknowledge your part in the grievance without justifying your part.
4) Say you're sorry.
5) Mean it. Apologizing is not about who is right or who is wrong. It is about resolution.
6) Learn.
7) Carry on without "carrying on".

DAY 249
DEBUNKING EVIL

Darkness exists. As does Light. However, Darkness is not the all-powerful force that we have made it to be. Many religions teach "clinging to God" in order to be "saved" from the "power" of Darkness. In fact, this ideology teaches that Dark is more powerful than Light and relegates Light as a default; this is a very crafty way in which to convince Humanity that we are helpless victims in a sea of sin and chaos. As long as we are distracted by a belief system that we are weak, not enough, and powerless, we choose separation from our Highest Design -- Light. Light is the most powerful force there is here on the planet Earth, as It designed not only us, but this third dimension in which we live. Though it can be challenging to encounter, Evil, or "The Devil", does not create stumbling blocks in our path. It is we who cause ourselves to stumble, adopting the decision that Darkness is the most powerful force there is. If you struggle with the idea that Darkness is following you, or that you cannot get out from underneath the mantle of Darkness, or bad luck, remind yourself: We have been brainwashed to believe we are not enough by those who require us to never open to our full potential. Should we open wide, those who maintain power through fear, restriction, and victimization will then lose their fulcrum for oppression. "The Devil" is not our worst enemy.

We are.

DAY 250
COMPASSION

Compassion is all about accepting that another's anger, hurt, pain, vitriol, ignorance, stubbornness, and fear is not at all about YOU. Step to the side of the wave of discontent that comes at you from another. Have compassion for the storm that rages within them that would cause such unrest.

Then thank Creation that it is not your storm to endure.

DAY 251
AUTHENTICITY

Authenticity is all we have. When we misrepresent ourselves to others, claiming we've had jobs we haven't, accomplishments we haven't, relationships we haven't, we are saying to the Universe: "The current version of who I am is not enough and I do not have the courage to become who I claim to be." The Universe simply says "Amen" to all of our proclamations, believing in our ability to choose our lessons. To live in authenticity with others, to embrace our strengths as well as our shortcomings, is to say to the Universe: "I am exactly who I am, right now."

And in the NOW is where all life truly happens.

DAY 252
SPEAK UP

When we don't speak out our needs, we are left feeling as though we are invisible. It is the responsibility of each one of us to bring a voice to the needs that we have. Most of the time we wait for those that we care about to notice that we need something and then go away disappointed and hurt when our needs are not acknowledged. Yet we hesitate speaking out our needs for fear of them being rejected, so we go away feeling rejected anyway.

Give your needs a voice and allow others the opportunity to rise to the occasion.

DAY 253
THE WAY

You are not a decision. You are. Love is not a decision. It is. Be what you are.

That's the way it is.

DAY 254
DECISION

Decision is action. Choose a situation in your life that no longer serves your highest well being and decide not to further participate with the energy of that situation. This decision does not have to be a dramatic external display. Decision is an internal gesture. Imagine a water faucet attached to your heart with a hose running out toward the situation that no longer serves you. This hose gives the negative situation water to grow. Turn off the hose and watch the water trickle to a halt. Then pull in your hose. Take the energy away from the situation that is being "watered" by your energy and turn your attentions to something you've always wanted to accomplish. Toss your hose in the direction of your dreams, goals, and aspirations and once again, turn on the faucet. Watch the water feed this new and fertile crop in your life. Focus on the growing of that yield alone.

Your life will change instantly, one sprout at a time.

DAY 255
WAKE

Wake up, you beautiful being. Thaw into who you are. Wipe the crust from your eyes. You're miraculous. You're created to do anything. You are anything. You are the creation of Creation. You are hostage to no one, beholden to no one. Wake and accept your lineage. The world needs you. You need you.

Wake.

DAY 256
SELF-FORGIVENESS

Though there is always room for improvement in each one of us, full acceptance of oneself involves self-forgiveness. It involves forgiving others, even if they have no idea we are harboring resentments. It involves extending grace (unearned slack) to ourselves and to others for any shortcomings. Self-acceptance starts with addressing our pitfalls and realizing that being human makes us human. Self-acceptance means that we stop beating ourselves up because we let ourselves down.

And, it means that we stop beating up those around us for not saving us from ourselves.

DAY 257
STAY IN EMPATHY

Always seek to maintain empathy. It is the glue which fastens us to the life process of others. The person who lacks empathy is incapable of putting themselves in someone else's shoes because they are wholeheartedly disinterested in anyone else's process but their own. Apathy is an ugly red flag that accompanies self-obsession, resentment, bitterness, entitlement, and blame. It's a cancer that slowly eats the soul. Once we lose our motivation to connect in empathy, we are truly an island, the stray Gazelle at the back of the herd while the rest hop onward, ripe for Darkness to pick us off.

In Apathy, no one can hear you scream.

DAY 258
GROWING MEANS LEARNING

We, as a species, are infinitely capable. We are capable of great bridge building with healing through accountability, and we are capable of great destruction through illusion. Our design as Beings of Light supports learning lessons in order to excel. We are meant to excel when we grow. We are meant to grow when we change. We are meant to change, period. We must choose whether or not we have the courage to change through accountability, or whether we wish to learn our lessons while fighting through the rabbit warren of complications created by our own illusions.

Either way, we learn.

DAY 259
RECIPE FOR PEACE

If the human race were ever to truly grasp how powerful we are -- our potential, our abilities, our true design -- we'd have no need for money. We'd have no need for jobs that did not fulfill the desires of our soul. We'd have no fear of loss. We'd be uncontrollable by a third party who relies on our addiction to the idea that we are limited in our resources, and that these resources can only be granted by a third party who wishes to keep us all in lack, limitation, and fear. We'd be free to focus not on survival, not on what we don't have, not on the self, but on developing systems that would continue to benefit the whole. If we are no longer addicted to the idea of isolation, if we no longer see ourselves as a lone soul against the world, then we become part of everything around us. We become the body of society. We become the blood of evolving and positive change. We *become* the beauty instead of striving *toward* the beauty. We no longer have need for stigma, for dogma, or for judgment. We'd only have the need to connect to All That Is, one another, nature, Universe -- God.

This is the recipe for achieving Peace on Earth.

DAY 260
WHY YOU COUNT

When you feel that you don't have any affect on the life around you, remember: We are spiritual creatures navigating a three-dimensional environment while seated in a space suit made of flesh. We bring miracles through empathy by offering a kindness to someone at a crucial time in their life, thus saving it. We exude joy into our environment thus giving others permission and safety to do so themselves. We choose hope which births hope in others. We pour enthusiasm into the stagnant pond, oxygenating the water with fresh possibilities. We restore dignity to the human spirit by soothing pain with compassion. We are hobbled by our own sorrow, giving others the beautiful opportunity to shine brightly as they reach to help us. We remain strong while the storm beats upon our shutters, sheltering those inside whom we would die to protect. We stumble until we fill the shoes we've chosen to wear, only to give away the same shoes to someone else in need once we've grown into a new pair. We recoil in fear so that others may teach us faith. We love, and we are loved.

This is how we affect the external world.

DAY 261
WHO YOU ARE NOT

Our desires originate from our heart. Yet if we become our desires and leave behind our heart, the foundations of our very endeavors are built upon the weakened sands of illusion. We have the opportunity to marry our Highest Design with our Deepest Desires if we keep our intentions pure in our pursuit of both, staying out of fear. If we step past the purity of honoring our Design and instead step into Ego (the state of allowing insecurity to replace confidence) our opportunities will fade as we teach ourselves who we really are by learning the hard way –

-- who we are not.

DAY 262
BE IN THE MOMENT

How do we chart our course, make our mark, enact our highest potential, and find our purpose and path, when so much of this incarnation is out of our control? It's simple. We must accept the fact that our highest design, purpose and path have nothing to do with the illusion of *control* at all -- but with sinking into the greater flow while doing what we love. When fishing while floating on a raft, we are not in control of the current, yet the raft is moving as we are casting along the banks. We are busy with the act of fishing, baiting our hook and tossing our lines. Yet we are not in control of where the fish may lie beneath the water or how quickly the current is moving us along. While we are on the raft, we are excited at the thought of the potential in every cast of the pole. We are not feeling "cheated" by the river as it "controls" our direction. We are not feeling "undermined" by the invisibility of the fish in the water. Our PURPOSE -- to fish -- is executed with utter joy brought on by nothing more than the act of fishing itself. It is all about the action in the moment.

So should we approach our life and the pursuits that we feel are in our highest good.

DAY 263
COCKTAIL FOR PURPOSE

Our Path and our Purpose are a mix of many things, much like a cocktail. Here is the recipe:

1 Ounce Faith
1 Ounce Courage
Jigger of Humor
Dash of Destiny
Cranbery Juice
Twist of Lime

Shake vigorously and serve over stone cold constitution.

DAY 264
RELEASING FEAR

The best we can do to assist someone who is drowning in Fear Consciousness is to address them with compassion. Anger against Fear brings out rage. Rage against Fear brings out Apathy. Love against Fear melts Fear. And once Fear is melted, the person who has been held captive in the lonely one-person cell within their own skin --

-- will emerge.

DAY 265
READJUST YOUR PERSPECTIVE

Financial duress is imposed by the mind, an addiction to a belief in lack and limitation. One million dollars starts with just one penny. Readjust your perspective and reach into your pocket.

You're carrying the seeds to a billion dollar bumper crop.

DAY 266
CHOOSING LESSONS

Humankind is not born "evil". We are simply born impressionable. Thanks to our spiritually genetics based in Light, we seek The Light, and in aligning with our Point of Origin, we are kept safe within a vibration of Light that Darkness will not dare penetrate. To align with The Light is to stand within a resonance that repels Darkness. If one is to take on selfless actions, one's selfless deeds will resonate with Light, creating a barrier that Darkness cannot cross. The war of principalities between Light and Dark, waged in the psyche of Humankind, is not our battle. We are simply the battle ground.

At times, we choose the lesson of becoming the collateral damage.

DAY 267
THE DYNAMICS OF DESPERATION

Desperation is more insidious than fear. Fears can be put to ease through education and applying oneself. Desperation cannot. It is an emotion that comes from twisting one's perspective so badly that the very path one is on becomes blurred into an irrational nightmare. It is an energy based on the illusion that "things will never get better". It is a subtle and powerful poison so private, isolating, and terrifying, that most never understand how deeply their life is affected. Desperation ruins friendships, business and personal relationships, and opportunities. Desperation fuels knee-jerk reactions. It creates prisons in our mind where there were formerly no walls. It creates a false sense of purpose within an individual ("I was so desperate to pay my bills that I robbed a bank.") Desperation is a trickster. It convinces us that we have no other choice, so the desperate choice we make is suddenly acceptable because we "had no choice". Desperation clouds our judgment. Desperation is the intersection where worry and hopelessness meet. Come out of relationship with Desperation.

It will never serve you.

DAY 268
CULT OF LIMITATION

Throughout history, human kind has suffered greatly at the hands of those who would exploit our most intense insecurities. We have been programmed into a Cult of Limitation for the sole purpose of placing our Light under a bushel. As long as we do not believe we are capable of shining, we won't. As long as we convince ourselves that we have nothing to offer, we will strive to offer nothing. As long as we believe that we are only capable of excelling to a certain point, we will fail to excel. We keep ourselves in boxes made of our own projected limitations because that is what we have been trained to do from a very early age. Yet we are not the sum total of our training. Break free from an identity that was never yours to begin with.

Excel.

DAY 269
HOW DO YOU LEARN?

Learning through fear is akin to staying engaged with the energy of the lesson over and over again because we're not ready to let go and move on. If we learn through selflessness, we give the lesson away by not needing to receive validation of our actions. If we learn through joy, we give the lesson away because it is replaced with joy. If we learn though love, we transform the lesson. If we learn through humility, we absorb and transmute the lesson.

If we learn through abandon, we turn the lesson into trust.

DAY 270
YOU MAKE YOUR WORLD

The first step in realizing our relevance in the world is in letting go of trying to prove who we are to the world. It is not the world's function, nor its job, to validate us. Yet we continue to seek a pat on the head from a system that has no hand with which to pat us and no heart with which to love us. As human beings, we personify everything around us in an attempt to understand it – including the world. We subconsciously view society as a parent figure, capable of making or breaking us with its support or reprimand. As such, we crumble into a crest-fallen mess, our feelings hurt because "our worth" has not been acknowledged by a system that was built not to nurture us as a parent would, but to sustain itself. Therefore, in order for us to truly understand how we each matter in the world, we must first stop being at odds with a system that is not at odds with us -- because it is not aware that we exist. Your world is exactly what you make it.

It does not make you.

DAY 271
CHANGING YOUR WARDROBE

Many of us attempt several different versions of ourselves throughout our lifetime, just like trying on different outfits. This is not indecision. This is growth. It is in this "experimentation of self" that the complex nature of who and what we are begins to form a very vague picture of our entire potential. Yet our potential is not a one-sided endeavor. In fact, our potential is maximized in the fact that we are, in no way, one-dimensional beings. Attempting to live one-dimensionally as a three dimensional being housing a fourth dimensional soul --

-- is the definition of confusion.

DAY 272
FEARING THE WORST

Fearing The Worst is a habit developed by attempting to recover from the pain incurred while enduring a challenging event for which we were not emotionally prepared. Once we recognize that Fearing The Worst is not about fear at all, yet about the need to identify the possibility that we will not be in control, then "fear" becomes debunked as an issue of preparation. There is a difference between being prepared and being made paranoid by life's uncertainty. If you find yourself falling into Fearing The Worst, remind yourself that your emotional reaction is not about Fear at all. You are simply untrusting of yourself to handle life's curveballs. Trust yourself.

You know what you're doing.

DAY 273
STUDY THE BLADE

Be mindful of your words and your actions. We cannot undo what we do, though it is possible for us to learn from the complications we compile while reacting to a challenging situation. We do not need to swing wide with our emotional baseball bat in order to protect ourselves -- though many of us do. We are trained to annihilate that which hurts us yet in doing so we often destroy the means to reconciliation. The very platform that launches the missile also protects the delicate flowers below from destructive flames. Resist the urge to destroy that which cuts you.

There are lessons to be learned by studying the blade.

DAY 274
RAWNESS

Making a true connection with another person requires allowing ourselves to be vulnerable on a level that often inspires greatly uncomfortable feelings in most people. Though we crave connection we fear vulnerability. We cannot truly connect with another unless we are able to connect with the Self. To do so, we must drop all walls that keep us separate from the parts of ourselves that we may not able to control, shine up, or edit. Our greatest strengths lie in our most raw areas. We crave the type of connection with another that allows our least polished places to be appreciated by the one who loves us. To truly connect with another --

-- we must first appreciate and accept our own rawness.

DAY 275
EXPECT TO NOT KNOW

The more prepared we wish to be from day to day, the more disappointed we are when life takes its own course. We forget in all of our planning that the Universe has its own design and its own pace. We also forget that the Universal design has a purpose past our own "To Do" list. If the entire Universe was meant to operate on only our best laid plans, it would be a very dull place indeed. Expect not to know what is going to occur day to day. Be okay with variance. Accept "curveballs" as "detours". The Universe isn't attempting to distract you from your plans.

It's attempting to fulfill them.

DAY 276
IT'S OKAY TO NEED

We are taught that unless we are independent, emotionally, we are weak. We are taught that we should not ask for help as asking for help is a sign of lacking independence. We are taught that needing the love of another is codependent. We are taught that wishing to be held in the arms of someone who loves us is "needy". We are taught that everything we naturally crave as a human spirit -- everything that our internal spiritual system requires in order for us to operate at peak capacity -- is frivolous. We are sold the idea of a stoic, isolated, financially strangled lifestyle and we wonder why we feel empty, hungry, frightened, scared, and unfulfilled. You're designed to need, while keeping "need" in balance with "want".

It is all part of how we learn to receive.

DAY 277
BE KIND TO YOURSELF

Be kind to yourself. If you are tired -- rest. If you are thirsty -- drink. If you are worried -- call a friend. If you are hungry -- eat. Moderation in all things is the key to not only balance, but also fulfillment. Society embeds ideals within us that are completely contrary to our design. We are to starve the body but feed the bank account, starve the soul but feed the guilt, starve the mind but feed the "drama". Nothing about starving is kind. We are not designed to have to endure suffering yet we often choose suffering, believing it is our only option. How would you fill your time -- if suffering were no longer an option?

It requires personal discipline not stop victimizing yourself.

DAY 278
TRUE RELEASE

The process of forgiveness is first and foremost about release. Before we are able to forgive others, we must forgive ourselves for our participation with them or with a situation that has caused us pain. It is in learning to forgive the Self that we are set free.

Not in the forgiveness of other's actions towards us.

DAY 279
THE DYNAMICS OF MARTYRDOM

Becoming a martyr is a cry for attention. It is the shot fired across the bow of insecurity, the failure in the heart to ask for that which is truly needs, the action taken in lieu of the solution. When we martyr ourselves, the energy of passive action becomes aggressive. Passive aggressive action nets frustrating results. Enacting martyrdom is energetically identical to attempting to run three horses in a race: Only one can win but all three require food, care, and someone to ride them, so the resources spent trying to cross the finish line don't justify the prize money. Instead of throwing yourself under your own bus attempting to prove a point to another -- simply speak your needs.

Find your voice.

DAY 280
LISTENING

When in doubt -- listen. We can listen with all six of our senses, not simply with our ears. Listening is the most important action we can take when attempting to figure out a challenging situation. Listen to your gut. Listen to the needs of those around you. Listen to what others are not saying when they speak. Then listen to what they are saying when they act. Listen to the space between receiving texts. Listen to the days between phone calls. Listen to your intuition. And above all, listen to your heart.

It speaks all languages.

DAY 281
WHAT IS ANGER?

Anger is not a negative emotion. It is often a flag that points us toward an area in which we, or another, are experiencing imbalance. By correcting the imbalance, we are able to set right our own course. Do your best to not become emotionally attached to anger. Healthy anger is a rooftop vent, a boundary-maker in disguise. Anger can be healthy when we are able to communicate the emotion with grace. When we are owned by anger, it is no longer simply an emotion -- but a behavior. When anger becomes a behavior, we are then on the other end of an agenda that has nothing to do with pointing us toward resolution. Anger as a behavior relegates us to becoming a puppet --

-- always mastered by Darkness.

DAY 282
I DON'T KNOW

Without the ability to accept information that we may not have authored, we lose the ability to adapt. Without our ability to adapt, we cannot grow. Our low ego craves being known as "the authority" on nearly every subject. The problem then becomes that most of us are not experts in one subject, let alone many. The greatest show of strength in any application is one's ability to say "I don't know". I Don't Know means "I am listening fully, and have enough respect for the situation to waste no one's time." Resist the urge to be an expert when you are not.

Always remember: The Low Ego is a pushy playmate.

DAY 283
FEEDBACK

The human species often desires feedback. It can be feedback on a project, feedback on a meal, or feedback on what was just said. When the desire for occasional feedback becomes a compulsion, the need is no longer about communication. *Craving* feedback is a sign of feeling invisible. A compulsive need to *give* feedback is also a sign of feeling invisible. If you find yourself driven to deliver unsolicited feedback on a regular basis, bring the application of feedback into balance by asking: Why *must* I voice my opinion? Will my opinion make a marked difference, or am I simply craving the opportunity to place the focus on myself? Conversely, if you find yourself driven to request feedback from everyone at every occasion, ask yourself: Why *must* I receive input form others, thus not trusting the value of my own decision? Feedback in moderation can be a fantastic learning tool. Out of moderation --

-- feedback is the crutch as we hobble on the broken ankle of life path impotency.

DAY 284
DULL THE BLADE

When stinging words cut your heart, treat not the wound --

-- but dull the slicing blade with non-participation.

DAY 285
ALWAYS ASK

Due to the fact that every human being views the world from a different perspective, we often find ourselves confused when communicating with one another. Moreover, we find ourselves inserting our own meanings into not only other's sentences, but their entire motives. This assumption behavior is a fear-based reaction to feeling out of control. The tendency to enact this behavior on a regular basis is an indication that we are not interested in the information delivered by another, but only interested in having an answer, even if it is incorrect. This compulsive need for answers is not about communication. It is about satiation. Instead of crumbling beneath our own lack of information in any given situation -- simply ask.

There is great power in clarification.

DAY 286
LOOK AROUND

Nature is a powerful demonstrator of all things possible. Wild animals survive the most intense winters and most arid summers, all the while not truly knowing where their next meal will come from or if they will find a mate. They don't have a 401K retirement plan and they haven't just refinanced their home at a better interest rate. We spend a great deal of time in worry about these types of these issues yet we forget that there is an entire world around us that operates at peak capacity for all life involved -- without our micromanagement. Today, remind yourself that the world in which you live is not designed by you. You simply manage your day to day tasks. The rest falls into place, by design. The system itself, in which you live, has been authored by a much more detail-oriented Universe and it's had billions of years to work out the kinks of cause and effect. You are amazing at what you do. Let Universe do what it does -- on your behalf. That's the design. When we put ourselves into perspective within the workings of the rest of the Cosmos --

-- it becomes easy to rest the spirit and the mind.

DAY 287
THE ILLUSION OF LONELY

One of the worst feelings is the blanket of loneliness that comes upon us at the most fragile hour. Loneliness is the most deceptive illusion of all. As beings who are infinitely connected by not only our spirits but by the very physics that hold together our three dimensional universe, we are always connected. Loneliness is a trick of the mind, inspired by the Dark, using our own arsenal of insecurities as fuel to propel us into a further state of isolation. Loneliness is a very real sensation, a yearning of the heart to connect. We fall prey to its grip when we forget that what we are FEELING in that moment is simply that -- what we are feeling. In that moment. It does not define the rest of our lives, nor does it define tomorrow. Close your eyes and remember that you are deeply visible to the Universe, right now. Deeply valuable to a timeline you may not even be able to comprehend in this moment. Deeply connected to everything around you even though you may feel that your needs go unnoticed. Hang in there. A hug is coming.

Your heart means everything to me.
-- The Universe

DAY 288
FINANCIAL FOOD

Money is an energy to which we have chosen to give great power. Instead of maintaining our spiritual birthright to infinitely create anything at any time, we have assigned away that super power to a piece of paper stamped with the image of a deceased Presidential figure. To put this into perspective, imagine having a table set with the perfect dinner. It awaits us to sit and partake. However, instead of sitting to eat what is already available, we go to the backyard, hungry, tilling the ground to plant the wheat to wait a season to harvest the wheat to grind the wheat to mix it with ingredients -- to make bread. We starve for a year when the banquet is still piping hot on the table. We do not believe the banquet is ours because we did not cook it. We do not believe it is real because we did not set the table. We only believe in the starving process because it is something that we can feel. We have been brainwashed to starve by those who wish to maintain control through managing our livelihood through controlling the flow of the paper containing the presidential portraits. Break the cycle. Wake up. There is a banquet on the table. You need not know who cooked it, or why. It is simply yours. BELIEVE there is ENOUGH for you, somewhere, in the Universe. Do not assign away your right to receive in ANY way that the Universe wishes to deliver your gifts. Money is not the only energy that represents provision. In fact, it is the least powerful of all the provision energies.

Now sit and eat.

DAY 289
TURN IT UP

The human body is over 65% water. Water is one of the most effective resonators on the planet Earth. Music -- sound waves -- literally ripple THROUGH the body. It's no coincidence that music is the language of the spirit, spoken by every living creature. Under a microscope, we are able to see that amoebas react to music. As do infants of all kinds -- human, giraffe, even fish. Allow music into your life and delight in its ability to heal, to inspire, to keep us company on a long drive, to hold us when we are feeling sad, to create a party where we have only malaise, to speak to us a language of Creation that we have forgotten, and to soothe us. Music is the Universal Balm. Always maintain music in your life.

Turn it up.

DAY 290
OPEN YOUR GATE

Let go. Whatever holds you captive -- let go. It is not an event, a person, or a place that keeps us imprisoned. It is our commitment to being the imprisoned person that locks the iron gate behind us.

Freedom is a decision, not a revolution.

DAY 291
CHECK YOURSELF

No one person is without fault. Check yourself. If you are being told repeatedly that you are exhibiting a behavior that others find challenging, it is not the job of the masses to understand your perspective. It is our job to smooth off the rough edges that snag the hearts and minds of those around us. This is one of our most profound lessons -- accountability and reparation. Before deciding that those around you don't understand your point of view, check yourself.

The truest strength lies in the ability to accept one's part in any debacle.

DAY 292
BEING EATEN

Giving away your ability to bring change into your life is much like allowing a piranha to gnaw on your ankle while wading in a cool stream. As we would kick away a toothy fish, we can also deflect the energies of those around us who wish to "eat" our life energies by enacting unrest, confrontation, and negative distraction from our Highest Purpose. Those who subscribe to a limitation consciousness do not believe that they can create their own flow of spiritual energy, or "food", yet their spirit must eat. To accomplish this, they often siphon the Energy of Possibility from those who allow Creation to easily flow through them. This is accomplished by initiating repeated negative interaction, an energetic exchange on a lower vibration that requires a great deal of focus from both parties. Though we should always respond to those who respectfully seek our assistance, be mindful of those who are too fearful to enact their own life purpose -- and must eat yours.

You are not an all-you-can-eat buffet.

DAY 293
ACCEPT

Accept love from all sources. Don't talk yourself out of it. Accept it.

Now go give it away.

DAY 294
HUBRIS

Pride is fickle. It will back us when our opinion matches with it's agenda. Once we decide that Pride must be replaced with Humility, it toughens it's skin and becomes Hubris. Hubris, unlike Pride, cannot be talked out of it's stance on anything. Hubris is unwavering, it's sense of dominion fueled by Pride. Once we allow ourselves to become the victim of Hubris, our judgment becomes deeply muddled. We monitor any situation through a lens whose only view is two inches in front of our nose. Hubris would have us believe this limited view to be Panoramic. The truth is, it's very difficult to appreciate any view --

-- from the bottom of our own emotional garbage can.

DAY 295
WHAT WE DO

Truth is what happens when Illusion ceases to fill our emotional needs. Evaluate what truly fills you. Be honest. Therein lies the answer to "why" we do what we do, day to day.

What we do designs our life.

DAY 296
MAINTENANCE

We limit ourselves because we fear the responsibility that we will inherit along with great advancement and success. Say to yourself: "If I am able to dream it, I am able to manage it." Because it's true.

We do not carry the desire of our heart without also carrying the ability to maintain it.

DAY 297
SPIRITUAL RECYCLING

Recycling can occur on a spiritual level as well. For instance, when chaotic energies begin swirling about you, imagine standing in a chamber full of 100 dollar bills that are being wind-blown all about. The rattle of the paper appears to be chaos, but if you simply reach out and snatch the refuse from the air -- what was once chaotic trash is now viewed as a one hundred dollar value. You can then utilize the energy that was once creating chaos all around you for whatever endeavor you see fit. Grab the chaotic energy out of the air and spend it as fast as you can. Don't duck -- pluck it up. Then re-invest your bounty.

Energy cannot be destroyed, only transferred.

DAY 298
LEAST RESISTANCE

Humanity personifies everything. We make every experience "all about us". We choose to make personal every action around us. Once we accept that the Universe does not serve us, but we serve the Universe -- we are then living in the True Design, rather than the design of our own making. The former is the path of least resistance.

The latter is the path of lessons through resistance.

DAY 299
CHARISMA DEFINED

Be the most charismatic person that you can be. It doesn't mean you have to be loud or extroverted. Charisma comes in many forms. Allow your spirit to shine, even quietly --

-- and you have bathed those around you in all that you are.

DAY 300
WONDER

The sea is filled with creatures we've yet to discover. The stars are mostly beyond our reach. We only understand a fraction of the human mind, and we are still not certain how bees are able to fly as their wings defy physics. We are not sure how jellyfish communicate and we are outdone, in terms of procreation, by frogs that are able to alter their gender at will. To say the world is void of mysteries is to completely misunderstand the world.

Embrace the mystery that is you.

DAY 301
PEP TALK

Never believe that you are powerless. That's a lie that Darkness throws around to see if you'll bite. Times may feel a little tough, but when the going gets tough, the tough look to people like YOU to see what course of action they should take. You have it together much more than you realize. You don't need to be perfect. You just need to BELIEVE in YOU. The rest will fall into place. Trust me. Why? Because you're worth it.

-- The Universe

DAY 302
PEACE MAGNET

No matter what is going on around you, only YOU have the power to control how you feel. When it all gets to be too much, close your eyes and envision how it would FEEL if everything were better. No pain, no struggle, no financial worries, no loneliness, no heartbreak. Now hold that feeling. Breathe into that feeling. Believe that feeling. Like Attracts Like in Spiritual Physics.

Create the vibration of peace, and peace will be drawn to you.

DAY 303
UNREST

Unrest in our life --

-- is nothing more than our spirit cleaning house.

DAY 304
SUCCESS MANAGEMENT

With great accomplishment comes great responsibility. Mostly, the responsibility entails upholding the ideals of the accomplishment that one has already agreed upon. The anxiety over freezing under the pressure of this "accomplishment maintenance" is often what we view as "Fear of Failure". Yet it's not failing that we fear but the maintaining of the achievement. Remind yourself that not only can you succeed --

-- but you can manage your success with ease.

DAY 305
CONTROL FREAK

The outward need for control is an indication that internally --

-- we have none.

DAY 306
LOVE FROM SUFFERING

Where there is great suffering, there is great opportunity for love to take root.

A church is never more full as when despair comes to visit.

DAY 307
NOTHING WASTED

Without exploring what we *don't* want, we often don't know how to ask for what we *do* want. Nothing in this life is wasted -- even our most painful experiences. As long as we're in movement toward understanding, no emotion is squandered.

We were born to recycle.

DAY 308
OUR PLAYGROUND STORY

Many millennia ago, the human race fell down on the beauty bark at the Universal Playground, and we caught a splinter in our palm. It was one of those really tiny splinters, the kind that you can't see with the naked eye, but you feel its white-hot sting every time you pet your cat. This splinter, otherwise known as Darkness, has interfered with our everyday activities every since. Every time we wash the dishes, that microscopic splinter flares up. Every high five, every handshake, every diaper changed, every pat on the back, that splinter sends a stab up our arm, reminding us that though it is invisible, it's lodged itself into our most utilized limb, and it's pain is part of our everyday life. A sliver is eventually doomed to be pushed from the body. As a foreign mass, the sliver will be evicted. The body will eventually eradicate any sliver by sending millions of white blood cells to surround the sliver, first soaking it to soften it, and then to push it toward the surface in a pressure pocket of white blood cells that gave their life to remove the foreign pest. Much like the white blood cells, the human race is flocking to the point of contact where the Sliver of Darkness has entered our Global Spiritual Body. We are throwing ourselves against the sliver to soften it – raising consciousness about world suffering, stepping back from corporate thievery, exercising social acceptance of those who may differ from us – all while placing pressure against the sliver to push it from our body. And, just like the white blood cells, some people are giving their life to become part of the pocket that pushes the sliver to the surface. Nothing is quite as tender, messy, or time consuming, as a sliver being removed by the body. So have patience. In the meantime --

-- keep pressing on.

DAY 309
NEVER ONLY ONE

The Universe will never force miracles upon us. We must accept everything that is to come our way. Challenge yourself to strike a healthy balance in both versions of yourself – The Super Hero and The Inner Five Year Old. Both of these people inside of you need to be free to function at 100% peak capacity, so they can each be readily available on deck to take their turn at helping you make key decisions. None of us are victims in our own lives. No one but you is in the driver's seat for your own journey. We tend to think that there is only ONE shot for us, ONE chance, ONE opportunity – because it is the only one that we can see at that present time. Therefore, we place all of that moment's value on ONE outcome. We panic if that opportunity does not fall to us. Or, we are devastated and enraged when we perceive that someone else has underhandedly "weaseled" our opportunity away from us. What is meant for YOU is meant for YOU. If we experience a "near miss" with an opportunity, watching it fall to another --

-- it is because it was simply never ours to begin with.

DAY 310
UNIVERSAL TIMING

The Universe is "air traffic control" for all things. As a passenger on the plane, if we were to take over the tower at LAX simply because we wished to land sooner, we would be responsible for the deaths of thousands of people on flights that we were unaware were even arriving. We must accept that in life, no matter how competent and fabulous and strong and calculated that we perceive ourselves to be — we are but a passenger on a larger vessel --

-- traveling at a velocity that is lethal for those to operate within who simply do not have the skill.

DAY 311
WHO ARE YOU?

In our body, blood courses through our veins. Yet we are not "blood". In our mind, dark thoughts sometimes occupy space. Yet we are not "dark". Our stomachs growl, yet we are not a "growl". The singular parts of what Creation is -- does not define It. It is not even it's singular parts made into one body that defines Creation. Creation is only defined by what It creates. As representations of this design, being made in the Image of Creation -- so are we. We forget that we are not what we create. We are so tied to the limitations in the physics of our three dimensional reality and so disconnected from our actual spiritual design (which has nothing to do with limitation) that we literally believe we become whatever it is we create -- the sales rep, the assistant manager, the mother, the father. We forget that every function we instigate is merely one aspect of the complicated puzzle known as Who We Are. We then struggle with feeling that all of who and what we are go completely dismissed. In fact, this perceived dismissal of who we are by those around us is mostly our fault as we assume the identity of only one aspect of our design.

You don't have to be a cake to bake one.

DAY 312
FEAR CONSCIOUSNESS

We can do our best to not engage the Fear Consciousness on a day to day basis. Like a virus or bacteria, Fear Consciousness an equal opportunity infector. We keep our spiritual antibodies strong by aligning ourselves with those who also seek Light, who live for the WE consciousness, not the ME consciousness. We align with those who understand communication and forgiveness. We keep up our spiritual immune system by aligning ourselves with God Energy -- meditation, prayer, writing a song, rocking a child, playing with a pet -- and by doing unto others what we would have done unto ourselves. We remind ourselves that our way is indeed, not the highway. And we trust. When we're hurt, we shake it off, and we still trust. And when we're disappointed once again, we realize it's not personal, and we STILL trust. Certainly, discernment is part of trusting. Yet there is no discernment in blindly adhering to Fear. Or Anger. Or Blame. Or Paranoia. Fear Consciousness is a spiritual sickness.

And it's treatable with Compassion.

DAY 313
YOUR CULTURE

Our feelings are often hurt when we feel that someone has not understood us. Yet would it not stand to reason that we, in that moment, then also do not understand the other person as well? Understanding of one another is not as much an issue of respect, but of culture. Just like cultures across the globe, each emotional culture has its own spiritual language. The Culture of Anger will not understand the Culture of Love. The Culture of Victimization will not understand The Culture of Accountability. The Culture of Violence will not understand the Culture of Peace. Each will find the other a complete mystery. Before deciding to participate with being wounded over another's perception of who you are, first define your own culture. Then ask yourself:

Do I speak their language?

DAY 314
MIRROR MOTIVATIONS

Being afraid is not a sign of weakness. However -- weakness is a sign of being afraid. Being in pain is not a sign of cowardice. However -- cowardice is a sign of being in pain. Struggle is not a sign of quitting. However -- quitting is a sign of struggle. Loving unconditionally is not a sign of commitment.

However, commitment is a sign of loving unconditionally.

DAY 315
WORTH

What are you worth? Your home, your car, your clothes, your land? What are you worth? Your dreams, your desires, your heart, your talents? What are you worth? Your ability to listen, to empathize, to support, to uphold? Now ask yourself:

What do I value?

DAY 316
VISION

Without our own vision of life, we are lost -- lost without action, without course, and without even the knowledge of what we have allowed to be stolen from us. Own your vision.

It's the one map that will never fail you.

DAY 317
ADDICTION

Addiction is the process of substituting one need for another. It is the distraction of the soul with an external substance while the internal world cries out for sustenance. We become addicted not only to drugs or alcohol but to behaviors that will substitute one item for one emotion -- work for fulfillment, food for sexuality, drama for intimacy, negativity for love. Addiction is the craving of that which we feel is the quick repair to a slow leak, a leak we have difficulty locating

Know your plumbing.

DAY 318
DEPROGRAMMING

We are programmed from the day we are born that we, on our own, are not enough. We are programmed that we must fight against life everyday we are alive, to scrap for what we get, no matter how dysfunctional. We are programmed with the idea of a god who only loves us if we act a certain way. We are programmed that at any minute, something or someone can swoop in and take everything we have. Conditions, conditions, conditions. The Cult of Limitation is only effective if its members all subscribe to the belief that they are completely powerless and completely inadequate.

Deprogram yourself.

DAY 319
IT IS TIME

It is time for you to learn the truth about who you really are -- a miraculous, powerful being capable of limitless creation by nature of the fabric of your very spiritual make-up. It is time for you to learn the truth about your real heritage, the spiritual gene pool that has birthed you in to a fantastic and unstoppable Miracle Machine. It is time to learn, and accept, what you are really capable of, in this lifetime and beyond. It is time that the invisible shackles come off of your wrists and the invisible fences stop blocking your path, leaving you open to wander in education, growth and enlightenment. Say it out loud: My life, as I know it, is only as real as I make it. I am real, and I must learn who I am, and use who I am without fear.

The time is now.
-- The Universe

DAY 320
FREE WILL CARD

Imagine sitting at a poker table. What if you always had an ace up your sleeve? You'd win every game. Technically, you have an ace up your sleeve, every moment you are alive. The Free Will Card is the unspoken pass that we can play whenever we wish in order to put our life, our identity, and our dreams back on track. It's a fabulous magic card, the "get out of jail free" card, much like the grandest permission slip of all time. This Free Will Card enables you to do anything at any time. Never hesitate to use it in a high stakes game, especially when you're ready to go all in.

But play it wisely.

DAY 321
REPROGRAM YOUR THINKING

The Top Ten Defeatist Mantras by the Cult of Limitation:

Cult Language: You have responsibilities.
Your Language: I fulfill all of my responsibilities with ease, in my own way.
Cult Language: That will never make you any money.
Your Language: Money comes to me easily in perfect order, in perfect amounts, when I perform my right tasks.
Cult Language: You need to stop being so selfish and think about your family.
Your Language: The desires of my heart define me, and are also my greatest personal contributions to my family.
Cult Language: What would your parents/neighbors/family think?
Your Language: I am not defined by my reflection in other people's eyes.
Cult Language: It's time to quit dreaming and grow up.
Your Language: As I grow older, I am even more capable of bring my dreams into reality, responsibly.
Cult Language: You have kids now so you need to plan for the future.
Your Language: I am teaching my children through example that they design their own future entirely.
Cult Language: You're too old to start again.
Your Language: I am wise through my many life lessons, and am even more equipped to begin a new endeavor.
Cult Language: You're delusional.
Your Language: I am able to see Reality for exactly what it is – an endless, boundless canvass that waits for me to create upon it.
Cult Language: How will you pay your taxes and where will you live?
Your Language: I am not fearful of loss because what is mine is mine by Spiritual Right, and what is not mine is not meant for me anyway.
Cult Language: You don't have the time.
Your Language: I make enough time for all things of value.

DAY 322
WATCH YOUR WORDS

Words, in their spiritual form, contain a vibrational frequency that sends up a flare so that the Universe may send along an outcome that is consistent with the vibrational request. Below, find a few commonly misused words and phrases that attract to their user a confusing outcome:

I BELIEVE means I SUMMON UNTO ME.
I WISH means IT IS NOT MINE ANYWAY
SOMEDAY means I DO NOT CHOOSE IT
I NEED means I AM WITHOUT ABILITY
YOU OWE ME means I LACK POWER
I AM AFRAID means I HAVE NO CONTROL
I CAN'T means I DO NOT OWN IT

To illustrate this confusion, let's look at the sentence, "I believe that someday I need to save up and buy a new car, but because you owe me, I'm afraid I can't right now, so I wish." In our three-dimensional language, the speaker seems like someone who desires to buy a new car but can't because of a pending financial problem. In our three-dimensional language, there is hope of a remedy in this sentence. The spiritual vibrational language of the sentence holds an entirely different meaning. It is this vibrational language that brings to us what we desire. Vibrationally, the sentence translates as: "I summon unto me that I am without ability to save up and buy a new car, but because I lack power, I have no control and I do not own it right now, so it's not mine anyway." The speaker has vibrationally told the Universe that they will not be getting a car. The Universe is bound by the laws of Free Will. If the speaker does not choose a car then the Universe cannot bring the vibration of "car" into the speaker's life.

Mind your words.

DAY 323
GET EXCITED

DON'T BE ASHAMED TO BE EXCITED! The Cult of Limitation teaches us a doctrine of limitation consciousness surrounding the idea of "getting your hopes up." We're taught that the higher our hopes, the greater disappointment. We're even taught that we can "jinx" our "good luck" if we get enthusiastic about something "too early". The Cult brainwashes us with the concept that to be excited equals great disappointment. Just like Pavlov's dogs, which automatically salivated when a dinner bell rang due to vigorous conditioning to the bell, we automatically stifle our own enthusiasm due to vigorous conditioning that enthusiasm = disappointment. This is yet another illusion spun by Darkness. According to Spiritual Physics, Like Attracts Like.

It stands to reason that the energy of enthusiasm is met with enthusiastic results.

DAY 324
PRESENT TENSE

Speak in the present tense. The Universe recognizes the term "someday" as, literally, some other day. To speak a miracle by saying "Someday I will have a high paying job", the universe must honor your request by continuing to deliver you "some other days". To say "I wish" means that the Universe must deliver to you only wishes, not results. And considering "I Wish" translates vibrationally to the spiritual language of "It is not mine anyway", your request is then negated. Speak out your desired miracle with confidence and in the present tense. This illustrates to the Universe that you do not place the limitation of denying the miracle by assigning it away to "some other days." If you want a new job right now, even if you have no logical line on a new employer, first put into place the energetic building block of belief.

This will usher in the opportunity much faster.

DAY 325
ALREADY HAPPENED

Accept the miracle you desire to experience as if it's already happened. This is extremely key to the manifesting process. We don't book a cruise and then call the travel agent every five minutes to see whether or not our reservation is still standing. We book our cruise and trust the travel agent to secure our reservation. We then let it go, with faith in our travel agent's ability to deliver. If we can have such faith in a mere person, then surely we can place more faith in the power of The Universe which flows through our veins. Speak out your miracle in the present tense then let it go. The Universe must deliver to us that which we choose to accept in the "now". To wonder if a miracle will happen, or to question when or how it will happen --

-- is to take the miracle off the table.

DAY 326
MEANING OF ACCEPTANCE

We're taught that to be accepting of a situation means that we are conceding to a situation and giving up a piece of ourselves in the form of our hard-earned opinion. We are taught that being accepting means that we are being violated. The goal of Darkness is to continue to convince us to stay isolated from our own greatest spiritual gifts and abilities. There is no greater way to achieve our isolation than to teach us that what is our greatest strength is actually a terrible weakness. A few common spiritual misapplications of the word "Acceptance":

Misapplication: I can't accept what he did to me
Perspective: His actions were hurtful towards me, but I, and my life, are not the sum total of his hurtful actions
Misapplication: I don't care if people are gay, but I can't accept homosexuality as a lifestyle and still be right with God
Perspective: I don't understand the dynamics of a homosexual relationship, but I do not allow my lack of understanding to threaten my spiritual path.
Misapplication: Her behavior is unacceptable.
Perspective: I am having difficulty understanding what has motivated her actions, and therefore, I am not equipped to engage what I do not understand.
Misapplication: If I accept what has happened, then I condone it.
Perspective: I recognize that I cannot change what has happened, and my approval or disapproval of the situation is irrelevant.

Acceptance is the energy signature that allows an incident to pass through us. When we personalize, or become, every aspect of an incident or someone else's process, we then willingly give away our own spiritual path for the moment and become a passenger on someone else's journey -- with no ability to affect the course of our ride.

DAY 327
WHAT IS LOVE, ANYWAY?

Love is not an ideal captured solely in the written works of poets and playwrights. Love is an actual, physical energy, a density. Love is the tangible, taste-able energetic connectivity that is hardwired inside each and every one of us, like the Universe's fastest Bluetooth connection. This connection allows all of us to experience harmony with one another. It allows us to step out of judgment. Judgment energy is fear-based and the weightiness of Love overwrites the weakness of the Fear-Based vibration. This process is often what we refer to in modern culture as "forgiveness", but more accurately, "forgiveness" is the process of allowing the Love vibration to attempt to occupy the same exact space as the Fear vibration. Light and Dark cannot be in the same place at the same time, so instantly, the energetic vibration of LOVE --

-- trumps all.

DAY 328
FORGIVE

Forgive.

You'll feel better.

DAY 329
REST

We grind ourselves with duty from dawn 'til dusk, laboring under the assumption that this action will somehow net us a better future. We forget that in the 24 / 7 running of our biological system -- we are meant to rest. Rest is not an option but an imperative. Spiritually, we rest in one another's support. Emotionally, we rest in the kindness of another. Mentally, we rest in silence. As a spirit in a human body, we are designed to experience downtime in order to process our daily events and recuperate from the day's challenges. Resting is not "being lazy".

It is necessary.

DAY 330
TOPCOAT

When angry words wish to fly from the mouth, turn them instead into tears.

Anger is the topcoat for the hurt that lies beneath.

DAY 331
DON'T FEAR SILENCE

Be thankful for the littlest of things. It is the tiniest of items that determine the strength in any given situation. Even the greatest titanium structure is made up of miniscule atoms, each atom being made up of 99.99999999% empty space. In a moving company's packing endeavors, it is the empty space between the packing popcorn that creates the "give" within the box that protects the items within. It is actually the empty space, the space in between all things, which creates its strength. We must have empty space within us to create to "give" in our life. If we pack in too many obligations, too many thoughts, to many worries, we lose our "give". Though we are all connected, we are also separate. That is the design -- to be ultimately connected and ultimately empty, all at once.

This is the beautiful mystery of being human.

DAY 332
CONNECT

We like to think of ourselves as independent. As a spirit and as a person, we indeed are independent of one another. Yet it takes a healthy dependency on one another in order to create a functioning structure where many dwell, such as society. We are not designed to be utterly solitary though many prefer their alone time. It does not compromise your independence to acknowledge that we all require others in our lives. In fact, it creates a greater strength within each one of us to know that even though we are independent of one another, our soul recognizes a union with another as "home". Don't allow negative feelings to choke out your need for others in your life. That separation is a lie of the Dark that seeks to keep you solitary. In prolonged isolation, we are at our weakest.

Connect.

DAY 333
DIVINE PROTECTION

The number 333 is a trinity number, the "God number", assigned its value by an Angelic system of language that is based upon numeric codes. An equilateral triangle is one of the most sturdy structures in home construction as all three angles support all three sides equally. So is it with us and the Universe. Our crossbeam fits perfectly into the bracket that The Universe supports, and our support fits perfectly into the bracket that Spirit Life supports. We are all intended to work together to uphold an entire system -- an entire structure -- around us. Today, recognize and accept that you are not only blessed with Infinite Support and Divine Protection by Universal Spirit around you --

-- but your very existence helps uphold many others in the Cosmos that you are not even yet aware.

DAY 334
MIN, BODY, SPIRIT

To heal the mind is to quiet raging storms. To heal the spirit is to return the voice to joy. To heal the body is to polish the floors of your own temple. Strengthening all three elements is necessary when overhauling the Self. We are a being in three parts -- the consciousness, the spirit, and the flesh. We cannot allow one area to fall into disrepair without compromising all areas. Though vastly different, they are all intimately connected. The Mind is the spark of the Spirit. The Spirit is the temperance for the Mind. The Body is the vessel for both the Mind and the Spirit, and the Mind and the Spirit help maintain the Body. We are a being in three parts, inseparable in our wellness, our illness, our growth, and our pain. You are a conscious, living machine. We honor our automobiles by scheduling proper maintenance.

Schedule your own maintenance as well.

DAY 335
RELAX

Breathe. Nothing can be done about yesterday. Tomorrow isn't here yet. The future is what you make it, and the past is an echo. "To Do" items on lists will still be there. The world will not cease to turn should you not text another right back. Emails wait patiently, dishes in the sink aren't going anywhere, and the laundry is neatly tucked in the hamper until it's done. So relax. There is nothing more destructive than the Illusion that indeed, we are completely captive to the duties in our life that were originally designed to make our life easier.

The tail does not wag the dog.

DAY 336
BE VIGILENT

Be vigilant in your quest for understanding. Many do not take the time to listen to another, nor observe the path which has wounded their feet. Be vigilant in seeking answers where others seek remedies. Many wish to only be filled yet contain nothing within with which to fill the cups of others. Be vigilant in comforting the broken hearted while others seek to satisfy their own needs. Many do not feel their pain. Be vigilant in your patience while the capriciousness of others tosses aside right action. Many are too impatient to realize the error in their judgment. Be vigilant.

Most are not.

DAY 337
ALLOW

When we clench our intentions tightly to our chest, we do not allow the Universe to bring us that which is in our highest interest. We demand of the Universe that it brings us that which we think will be in our highest design. Our thoughts and life plans may come from the right place within our heart, yet when we become inflexible to the idea that there may be other available options for us, we are limiting the Power of Creation. Remember, the Universe waits upon our Free Will. If you decide that there is nothing better for you, in life, then The Universe will deliver you the lesson of limitation with a firm "Amen". This is not a punishment from The Universe, but The Universe having enough faith in you to honor your decisions. Allow The Universe to be magnificent and to bring you miracles. The first step is accepting the POSSIBILITY that your life can be different.

Allow that acceptance.

DAY 338
PROBABILITY

To create a 24 hour day, the Earth is turning at 1000 miles per hour. To create a year, the Earth is rotating around the sun at 67,000 miles per hour. Surrounding the Earth are 29,000 pieces of space junk larger than 10 cm, 670,000 pieces larger than 1 cm, and more than 170 MILLION piece of space junk larger than 1 mm. This space debris has a total mass of more than 6,300 TONS and can travel as fast as 35,000 miles per hour. At that velocity, even a 1 millimeter object can pierce the hull of a spaceship. And we've yet to be destroyed, here on Earth. If The Universe is able to successfully navigate a planet holding 365 billion people and countless other life forms through an obstacle field of this magnitude, at this velocity --

-- then The Universe is most definitely capable of helping you navigate around your own speed bumps, at your current velocity.

DAY 337
PERSEVERANCE

An ant is capable of lifting an object 50 times its own bodyweight. If humans had this capability, we would be able to lift an automobile over our head. Ants were the first farmers, dating back to the Tertiary period 70 million years ago. Even though they are much smaller than we are, the total biomass of ants on earth equals that of all the people on earth, as there are roughly 1.5 million ants per person. Do we learn from such perseverance? We step on them, as children we fry them under the focused beam of the sun through a magnifying glass, and we poison their colonies. Perhaps we are simply jealous that a species we consider so inferior to ourselves outranks us in community, perseverance, and ingenuity. If the tiniest of ants can persevere --

-- so can you.

DAY 340
SUNSETS

The light from the sun changes as it dips to the horizon. It bathes the world in a peach or purple hue, softening the harsh edges of our reality. Nothing beneath this light has changed except for the color itself. The passage of time allows this blanket of light to cast the world in a different glow. And the glow itself is created from the refuse and dust kicked up into our atmosphere by the billions of us living below. If the sun is able to repurpose our atmospheric pollution for such beautiful outcome, have faith that the emotional and spiritual "pollution" in your own circumstance has the possibility to change the color of your surroundings in a beautiful way --

-- by allowing enough time for The Light to angle itself properly in your life.

DAY 341
DENTS

We become crestfallen when our most heartfelt pursuits are derailed by exterior circumstances. In fact, there is no such thing as an "exterior" circumstance. Though we are separate beings living amongst one another and surely, other people's chaos intersects our lives, we are designed to spring back from obstacles. We are impacted by a challenge. We proceed forward now sporting dents from the impact. These dents change our shape. What seems disabling at the time then becomes an asset later in life, as the bullet shot directly at us does not impact us --

-- but misses us completely as it passes through the dent in our side.

DAY 342
WIND

The wind blowing through the trees is invisible. We are alerted to its presence because we feel the movement through our hair and we watch the branches sway. We gauge the severity of the wind based upon the bend of the treetops. The wind itself has no mass. It has no form. It has no body. Yet it is able to bring both great ease and great destruction to the world -- as a gentle breeze on a stagnant summer night and a great roaring tornado, ripping the earth. This formless, faceless, bodiless, egoless energy shapes the planet with no agenda, no life path trajectory, no wants, no desires, no disappointments, no hopes, and no dreams. The wind is pure energy, demonstrating to us on a daily basis how a pure energy itself is capable of shaping our physical environment. All energy on Earth is accessible to all creatures. We all draw upon the same Source. The wind simple IS.

Now imagine what YOU can do, with focused intention.

DAY 343
HAPPY

    Allow happiness. There is no other "shoe that is going to drop". Not unless you wish it, to learn from the experience of disillusionment. Allow happiness. It's okay to let your guard down and be joyful. This is your nature. Allow happiness. There is no reason to perpetuate the myth that life is full of pain, simply because you have experienced pain. Defying happiness as a defense mechanism only wounds our soul, as our spirit craves levity and ease. Allow happiness. Do not chase it. It is not evading you.

    It is within you.

DAY 344
RIGHT NOW

Be still. Within the stillness is the gift of RIGHT NOW. Within RIGHT NOW is the answer to all of your concerns. RIGHT NOW will hold a conversation with you about what is actually occurring. Usually, what's actually occurring is not nearly as dire as our perception of the situation, once we remove all the worst-case possibilities of the future and the pain from the past. Being present, being in the now, is difficult in our very technological age. The addiction to distraction within humanity is at an all-time high. We encounter stillness and automatically reach for texts, social media, and email. We are so inundated on a regular basis with an endless stream of chatter that just as a dog conditioned to sit when a whistle blows, we react without thinking to the option of distraction. Distraction is one of the greatest tools used by Darkness to keep us waylaid from our path.

Be still.

DAY 345
OWN IT ALREADY

When confused about how to proceed forward, always go backwards. For instance, if you wish to have a new home, picture the home in your heart as if it were yours. Own it already. If you are concerned about the difficulty of moving, picture the ease in which friends and family help you package your goods, as if a fond memory. Own it already. If you are concerned about qualifying for the loan to obtain the home, picture the loan approval in your heart. Own it already. Our future is made up of the steps we take in the NOW in order to reach the point on the timeline that we would consider the future.

It's yours already.

DAY 346
GIFTS

The Universe is full of gifts that are intended for our use. Yet we are conditioned to only retrieve a gift on which our name is included. What we often fail to realize is that the gifts with which The Universe wishes to provide us, contain the names of many. We cannot steal a gift from another, nor can another steal a gift from us. We share many gifts and talents. It is our Illusion of Lack in this incarnation that spurs our feelings of jealousy and competition. Your gifts are your gifts, utilized uniquely by you alone. Though shared by many, your gifts would not be utilized by another in the way that you would apply them. It is in the application of your gifts that your true uniqueness shines.

Not in the gift itself.

DAY 347
VULNERABILITY

To protect the heart is to place a tourniquet on the soul.

The spirit turns black from a lack of circulation.

DAY 348
GIVING

We have learned from a young age that it is better to give than receive. Truly, it is not "better", but more fulfilling. From a Spiritual Physics standpoint, it is more functional as well. When we give to another, we send a message to The Universe that we do not fear lack or limitation. The Universe is designed to bring to us that which we think about. When we fixate on our fears, The Universe must bring us our fears. That is what we have requested by our action of fixation. To give is to say to The Universe: "I do not fear the loss energy, objects, or opportunities." The Universe is then bound to deliver you more energy, objects, and opportunities.

Thus defines the ideology: "You Reap What You Sow."

DAY 349
WASTED TIME

There is no such thing as time wasted. We are born into a flattened and three dimensional realm where our perception of time is linear -- one hour after the next, one day after the next. In Western Culture, we place events in an order based upon what happened "first", and what happened "last". We fixate on dates and deadlines. We start school when we are five. We retire when we are 65. Our weekend begins on the sixth day of the week. Within Indigenous Cultures, the idea of time is not related to the date on which something occurs, but related to the place in which the events themselves took place. If a Cheyenne Warrior was honored with becoming chief, it would not be the "date" of the occurrence that would be remembered, but the prairie on which his vision was received. If you fear that you have "wasted time" in your life in getting to the emotional, spiritual, and physical place you are today, remember: You are in the right PLACE

Therefore, you are IN YOUR RIGHT TIME.

DAY 350
HELPING

Assistance is an intention. When we assist another we must first make room in The Self to be able to shoulder the weight of another's challenge. Making room in The Self is much like cleaning up the living room prior to guests arriving. We must place to the side the incidental clutter of our week piled thoughtlessly in our living space in order to make room for others to sit. To assist another is the process of placing to the side the clutter that will consume our mental living space, cleaning up and prioritizing our own daily confusion. If you are finding yourself "stuck" in life -- assist another.

Helping another then helps The Self.

DAY 351
LOVE

    We claim to "fall in love", as if love were a pit. We claim to "find love", as if it were missing. We claim to "give love", as if it belonged to us. We claim to have "lost love", as if it were an object. Love is a noun, a verb, an adverb, and an adjective. It is applicable in all aspects of every situation possible across every culture, species, and genus. Love is not only the Universal Language --

    -- it is the Universal Ingredient.

DAY 352
HAUNTED

Memories are a trove of emotions. Our memories can be our greatest asset or our most terrifying captor. Playing on a movie screen within the mind, our memories encapsulate the experiences of our soul and our heart. In turn, our memories often weigh in when we are defining our identity. Are we the high school quarterback who brought home the state championship? Are we the survivor of great abuse? Memories provide us with a delicate balance between factoring in our identity from our past with who we are today on our current life path. If you find yourself haunted by memories, remind yourself that though valuable to the evaluation of The Self, your memories are simply bookmarks in your current development. Nothing more. Though memories may hold valuable keys to why you have taken your current life path, they do not define your development or accomplishments. Only your current daily actions define you. You are far greater than the sum total of your history. In fact --

-- you are actually made up of Pure Possibility.

DAY 353
CHALLENGE IN PERSPECTIVE

The greatest challenge of all --

-- is to live for more than the challenge.

DAY 354
ENLIGHTENMENT

Spiritual enlightenment does not have an end point. It is not a college course or a class to be passed. It is not a marker of superiority or a goal to achieve. There is no such thing as a more enlightened or less enlightened person, as enlightenment cannot be measured on a scale. Spiritual enlightenment is the process of releasing the definition of The Self while feeling defined by a greater connection to The All. There is no greater form of enlightenment than humility.

Ego is a sign of a soul who fears The Light.

DAY 355
CRITICISM

Be open to constructive criticism. Enact strength of character to learn from what resonates with you, especially if it is embarrassing, painful, or difficult to hear. Even if the commentary does not resonate with your experiences or opinion, be open to the fact that someone else felt the need to share. The karmic experience of "criticism" may not be about you at all, but about the other individual who is insisting on bringing forward their opinion. Those who offer obsessive feedback are seeking validation of their own life journey. Those who criticize simply to criticize are proclaiming that they are frightened of the uncertainties of life. Criticism is very often rarely about us but a statement about the other person who feels the need to express their opinion with us. Criticism is an effective self-evaluation tool for which we are given the opportunity to ask ourselves:

Do I trust myself to know my own truth?

DAY 356
DIRTY

There is more life in the first six inches of topsoil than on the entire surface of the Earth. So it is with our own spirit. There is more activity just beneath our own surface than in the sum total our exterior life. Never be afraid to dig into your soul and get dirty.

It's where the good stuff lives.

DAY 357
PERSPECTIVE ON CHANGE

There is change in your pocket. There is the change in the dressing room. There is change in your mind. Why do we fear change when everyday, it surrounds us? Put change into perspective. We do not fear change. We fear the idea of not being able to handle that which change brings upon us. You can handle anything. Especially that which you're certain you cannot. The most important change of all --

-- is the change you allow in your attitude.

DAY 358
I CAN'T

The human spirit translates for the human psyche:

"I Can't" means "I Won't".
 "I'm too busy" means "I won't make time."
"I'll never" means "I don't believe"
"I don't believe" means "I've been hurt."
"I've been hurt" means "I've been hurt."

Listen when another voices their pain. There is great honesty and courage in the vulnerability required to re-open a wound half-healed so that another may examine the depth of the carnage --

-- and learn.

DAY 359
FINISH

Finish what you start. We concoct many excuses in order to leave projects unfinished. The problem with this action lies in the message it sends to The Universe. When we do not complete a task, it not only weighs upon our mind as "unfinished" but it creates a leak in our energy and intention field. When we begin a project, we allocate energy into the Universe to bring that project into fruition. Universe then moves that project into the belly of our ship, to be transported to its destination and assembled. We cannot "take back" that intention once it is loaded, as energy cannot be destroyed, only transferred. In the case of an unfinished project, imagine a ship at sea whose forward progression has been slowed. We find what is weighing the ship and we fill a net with the extra cargo found below. Instead of making the port to which the cargo was destined to be unloaded, we attempt to take a short cut. We wrap the cargo in a net and kick the net off the edge of the boat. Suddenly the net is caught in the ship's rudder and our forward progression is slowed further. Any action which we have pledged to execute, whether it's painting the house, finishing a college degree, or cleaning the garage -- is an action tucked in the hull of our ship. The only way to energetically offload that cargo is to finish the project.

Don't waste countless gallons of emotional and spiritual fuel hauling a bulging hull.

DAY 360
NEGATIVE ATTENTION

Many people are raised in a family that discourages authenticity and emotional intimacy. When they are beset with an opportunity to connect with another-- they then lack the tools to recognize the most base of all connective modalities: Acceptance, love, compassion, understanding, and grace. Instead of relying upon the aforementioned emotional bridges, those who have not been modeled such forms of communication seek to fill up their emotional storehouses with negative attention. Many substitute "drama" for "intimacy". Initiating this negative action brings upon the individual more negative action, igniting the self-fulfilling prophecy of "always being alone". Drama within a relationship is not a sign of interest by another. It is a sign that one or more parties within the relationship are wishing to explore the more challenging aspects of The Self. Experiencing drama within a relationship has nothing to do with the relationship at all. It has to do with the emotional development of the individuals enacting the drama.

Emotional Intimacy should not hurt.

DAY 361
COOKING

The mincing and blending of edible ingredients is an art form. Part intuition, part science, part math and part practical application, cooking is about the dance between heat, chemistry, and intention. Intention plays a vital role. The same cookie recipe can be prepared by three different people in three identical ovens using identical ingredients -- and each batch will taste differently. Our intention flavors everything we "cook up" in life.

Always add love as a top tier ingredient.

DAY 362
WATERING THE PLANTS

Plants require sunlight and water in order to extract nutrients from the soil. Fish require oxygenated water in order for their gills to function properly. Human beings require water over food. The Earth continues to bathe itself in water so that all species may flourish. Water is the staple of all life. It falls from the sky. It cascades down our mountains. It feeds our skin, our soil, and our soul. It is the most important common element on this planet. And it is free. Our priorities have been distorted and our sense of provision has been replaced by a fear of lack. Do not struggle with the idea of what you do not *have*. What you *need* is freely given to you.

Just listen to the rain.

DAY 363
SHADOWS

A shadow is created when a solid object blocks the light. A shadow is then cast upon a wall, a mere outline of the complicated mass that created it. When we treat others according to our idea of what they are rather than taking the time to know who they are, we are attempting to befriend a shadow, the best parts of the individual catching the light. Do not enact shortcuts in the understanding of those in your life. They have been placed in your life so that you may learn from the complicated details that design their terrain. You yourself are far more complex than a mere silhouette.

Never allow your perceptions of another to block their light.

DAY 364
CAST IRON

To cook with cast iron is an exercise in commitment. One must accept that the iron itself, not the burner, is the source of heat. Though the burner temperature may be adjusted, the cast iron within the pan will maintain its own temperature. To cook with cast iron is to commit to the level of heat beneath the meal. Like a Dutch oven -- our spirit is cast iron. When heat is applied beneath us, we take on the heat, scalding everything around us and requiring time to cool off. Be mindful of where you place yourself, aware of your propensity to absorb the heat around you.

Once heated, we all take awhile to cool down.

DAY 365
TRANSCENDENCE

The one aspect of life that is unfaltering is your ability to change. Accept this ability. Rejoice in this ability. Your ability to adapt is legendary amongst the stars. You aren't expected to make a change overnight. Nothing is expected of you. In fact, you are perfect, just the way you are. I wish you thought so. I hope you're getting there. Until you get there, remember that everything you touch is a miracle because the fact that you are here -- is a miracle. The mathematical odds of ten millions sperm hitting the one right egg so that you may walk the Earth today are astronomically low. Yet here you are. Reading this. And that makes me really happy. Because I love miracles. I hope someday you figure out how to love yourself --

-- as much as I love you.

With Love Always,
The Universe

ജ❖ൽ

ABOUT THE AUTHOR

Danielle Egnew is an internationally renowned Psychic, Medium, and Author, known for her extensive work with spiritual education and Angels. She has appearing on and hosted several TV and radio programs (ABC, NBC, USA, TNT, LA Talk Radio). In 2012 she was chosen as "Psychic of the Year" and "Most Noted UFOlogist" by best-selling paranormal magazine *UFO's and Supernatural*, sharing a cover with noted Physicist Stephen Hawking and Syfy's Amanda Tapping (*Sanctuary / Stargate*).Her book *True Tales of the Truly Weird*, a memoir of her most bizarre paranormal experiences, debuted on Amazon's Top 20 list in the paranormal genre for over three weeks. Her feature-length documentary film *Montgomery House: The Perfect Haunting* in which she starred as well as produced and directed, has been referenced in the paranormal industry as one of the most thorough paranormal documentaries to date. A vetted alumni member of the national missing person's crime solving *Find Me* organization and *America's Best Psychics*, Danielle continues to work in media as a Psychic and Medium, even as a content consultant on many popular TV programs such as CW's *Supernatural*, Lifetime's *America's Psychic Challenge*, TV production companies and networks including The History Channel, and the blockbuster film *Man of Steel*. She currently anchors her own private Spiritual Practice in Big Sky Country of Billings, Montana while working in media abroad.

CONNECT WITH DANIELLE EGNEW

Official Website - www.DanielleEgnew-Advisor.com
Facebook - www.facebook.com/danielleegnew.psychicmedium
Facebook - www.facebook.com/danielleegnew
Twitter - twitter.com/danielleegnew
Blog -'The Call To Light Press' - www.CallToLight.org
YouTube Channel - 'The Signs and Wonders Network' -
www.youtube.com/user/danielleegnew

OTHER BOOKS BY DANIELLE EGNEW

True Tales of the Truly Weird:
Real Paranormal Accounts from a Real Psychic
Nonfiction, 173 pages

"This woman is the Real Deal. Wit, sensibility, charm and true ability. Read her book." -- Kim Rhodes, Actress (CW's 'Supernatural')

Truth is weirder than fiction. From Ghosts to Demons, Extraterrestrials to Kachinas, Banshees to Elementals, talking plants to people who cannibalize another's liver, renowned Psychic / Medium and Paranormal TV, Radio and Film host Danielle Egnew (ABC, NBC, TNT, USA, LA Talk Radio) has encountered it all -- sometimes with more terror than triumph. Uncover secrets of the magnificent yet monstrous unseen world that surrounds us everyday, recounted in exquisite and disturbing detail as experienced first-hand through Danielle's extraordinary Psychic abilities. At the heart of the chaos, take a rare and candid look into the life and psyche of one of today's most influential Spiritual and Paranormal personalities. An engaging yet chilling memoir underscored by fascinating history, harrowing humor, and freakish facts, True Tales of the Truly Weird is a powerhouse ethereal expose on what's really lurking beyond our comfortable realm of understanding, redefining our reality. The question is: Are we ready for the truth?

Available in print from Amazon, on Kindle, Nook, iBook, and many other e-readers. For links to retail outlets for easy online ordering, visit www.DanielleEgnew-Advisor.com